THE UNTOLD STORY

OF

OLIVE OSMOND

BY HER SON

VIRL OSMOND

The Untold Story of OLIVE OSMOND

Knowledge Unlimited, LLC
George Virl Osmond, Jr.
P. O. Box 942
Pleasant Grove, UT 84062

**KNOWLEDGE
UNLIMITED**

Cover Design by Chris Trainor

ISBN: 978-1-57636-189-4

Printed in the United States of America.

ACKNOWLEDGEMENTS

I wish to thank my wife, Chris Osmond, for her help in compiling and writing this book. She spent long hours interviewing me and going over my mother's journal and my journals with me. She typed and edited and helped me to tell this story in the way that would best honor my mother.

I want to thank my buddy, Alan Richards, for the hours of work that he put into compiling and organizing the materials from which much of this book was written.

I also wish to thank my friend, Pam Blackwell, for her publishing help and writing experience that helped me to bring this book to fruition. She has believed in my project for a long time and has encouraged and helped me every step of the way. She is a fine novelist and playwright. You can see what she has written at onyx-press.com.

TABLE OF CONTENTS

OLIVE & VIRL – 1976

OLIVE & VIRL – 1988

PROLOGUE

My angel mother, Olive, wrote quite a lot of material about her life, beginning with her early days in Idaho, through forty-plus years of show business, even up to a few weeks before her passing in 2004. The most consistent volume of writing was from 1970 when she wrote in her personal journal nearly every day. Many were one-line sentence entries, like "Pat Boone brought us a ham." Or "We got to meet Queen Elizabeth after the show." Or "Donny's single, 'Puppy Love' was at #1 in Brazil." And "...went to Merrill's apartment where we camped out, sang and told stories into the night." But other earlier entries were more deeply personal and spiritual in nature.

My mother was known to fans worldwide not as Olive, but as "Mother Osmond." She was a gentle, caring and compassionate woman, who had a capacity to reach out and genuinely love each person that she met.

This resulted in everyone calling her, "Mother," and meaning it in the deepest sense of the word. What is not evident from both her writing and her public appearances is the depth and breadth of her mind and soul. For example, one entry said, "I read some more in Tolstoy's *What Is Art?* and another, "I discovered a beautiful story of repentance in Victor Hugo's *Les Miserables*."

Reading was life to my mother. From Norton's *Anthology of Literature* to a text, *The American Experience*, to Durant's *Caesar and Christ*, she was an eager learner and ever-hungry for knowledge. She also consumed the scriptures, reading and studying them continually, to her delight.

Her motto was a Latin saying: "Petimus Altiora" ("We seek after higher things.") This became our family motto. She always encouraged us to read the best and learn from the best and thus do our best.

I was fortunate to be the first-born of my mother's children and her close confidante for many years. Because my brother, Tom, and I were born hearing impaired, she spent many extra hours working with us so that we would learn to talk and develop other skills that would help us live in a hearing world. She also taught us to play the piano and the saxophone and made sure that we had every opportunity to develop our talents. At the end, I cared for her the last two-and-a-half years before her death when she struggled with the limitations left by her stroke. Because of this close association, I had access to a deeper spiritual and emotional level of my mother, one that I want to share with the world. She was (and she still is) a remarkable, devout woman of faith, filled with love and light.

In Loving Memory of
Olive May Davis-Osmond

"I have no greater joy
than to hear that my children walk in truth."
3 John 1:4

OLIVE MAY DAVIS, AGE SIX MONTHS

CHAPTER ONE
BEGINNINGS

I watched my mother's face as we stood on the sidelines of the Andy Williams Show, waiting for my four brothers to make their entrance. It was December, 1962. Overhead lights and wires hung precariously. Huge cameras focused on the stage from every angle, and an anxious audience waited for the show to begin. The boys paced nervously, but Mother was very still and calm. She knew what this moment meant. Years of encouragement and hard work were to pay off. The talents of her sons had been acknowledged, and a choice window of opportunity was opening up. In a few moments, the world would know what she already knew. This was the beginning. This was the destiny that had played out in her heart and mind for many years.

"You have a special mission," she would tell my brothers. "God gave you this talent for a reason. Prepare yourself, and the opportunity will come." And now, it was real.

BEGINNINGS

Did she know that the destiny that drove my brothers would also propel her? Was she aware she would no longer be just a mother of nine children but would become the mother of a talented group of performers, who would become known worldwide? Could she see that she too would evolve into a public figure known as Mother Osmond? I could only see this single moment, but Mother saw the future.

Olive May Davis was born in her grandparents' cabin in southern rural Idaho on May 4, 1925. I do not know how many people were still being born in cabins in 1925, but she was. This birthplace helped develop deep familial roots and beliefs that were ever-present in her subconscious and established a foundation for her twentieth-century Mormon life.

Mother had a rich pioneer Mormon lineage. Her maternal ancestors heard Latter-day Saint missionaries on the streets of Durham, England in the 1860's. They sold everything they had and boarded a ship for the precarious trip to America. First they arrived in New Jersey and then traveled to a mining settlement in Coalville, Utah. The Mormon prophet, Brigham Young, had called for church members with mining experience to move and settle there.

My mother's maternal grandparents, Benjamin Thomas Nichols and Olive Lovenia Booth, were extraordinary people who were on call constantly to help heal the residents in the mining towns where they lived. People preferred calling them instead of the local doctor. In their cabin they kept on the top shelf of their pantry all the necessary pharmacology for a rural area clinic: consecrated oil, camphorated oil, mustard and clean cloths (for mustard plasters) and clean, white sheets to make the beds of the sick.

During the flu pandemic of 1918, the two were at the bedsides of many of their neighbors. When their own family became ill, Benjamin Nichols separated the sick members of his family into an empty adjacent house, while his wife continued applying her mustard packs and lemonade. None of their family members succumbed to the flu, whereas fifty to one hundred million people died worldwide.

Grandfather Nichols was a religious and faithful man. He believed in the power of prayer. When he laid his hands upon the heads of the sick and anointed them with consecrated oil, both he and those that were ill believed that they could be healed by the power which came from his priesthood and the faith which he had.

Her Welsh paternal ancestors followed nearly the same path—first to Pittsburgh to work in the coal mines. There they raised the money to make their way across country to settle with the body of Latter-day Saints in

Utah. Some time later her widowed grandfather built up a homestead in the little town of Samaria, near the Utah-Idaho border.

Her paternal grandparents were Samuel W. Davis and Mary Ann Martin. Both were natives of Samaria and also new converts to the Church of Jesus Christ of Latter-day Saints. Their parents had settled there from Wales. They too had a rich history of strength, hard work, and commitment to family and faith.

Samaria received its name when, in 1869, Lorenzo Snow, an apostle of the LDS Church, traveled to the rural outpost to scout out a location for a new Mormon settlement. He was so impressed with the kindness and hospitality of the current residents that he called them Good Samaritans, and thus the town was christened after that biblical story. I think it more than a coincidence that Mother was born into such a setting. I think she soaked up that atmosphere as a child, so that she could radiate those qualities as she traveled worldwide.

The town of Samaria is centered in the fertile Malad Valley at the base of the beautiful Samaria mountain range. The rolling hills seem to enfold and contain the valley, much like a mother's embrace. The winter storms that seem to bedevil other parts of southern Idaho seem to be tamer here. The land is irrigated so that Samaria, which sits in the center of the valley, appears as daubs of emerald green when one first enters the area. On a warm summer day, the air is pungent with the smell of alfalfa and hay. Grasshoppers occupy swaths of road and easement. This verdant, peaceful place had just one main road in 1925, when my mother was born. It ran past the church and general store, then wound its way to Malad City, ten miles to the north.

Like so many Mormon settlements that sprang up after the Church's migration to the Salt Lake Valley, Samaria was settled by persecuted Latter-day Saints who had been driven from their homes in Nauvoo, Illinois in the winter of 1846. Although their beliefs were basically Christian, members of surrounding religions were suspicious of them, their rapid growth in numbers, and the vibrant leadership of their founder and prophet, Joseph Smith.

This was not their first exodus. They had been cast out, hunted, robbed and murdered in large numbers from 1830 to 1846 as they ran from Palmyra, New York to Kirtland, Ohio, from the northern counties of Missouri where the governor signed an extermination order to get rid of them, and then on to Illinois, where they built Illinois' second largest city along the banks of the Mississippi River.

But the persecutions intensified, and within a few short years Joseph Smith was slain by a mob. They then were driven out of their beloved city, crossing the frozen Mississippi River with little more than the clothes on their backs. Destitute, they camped in Iowa while they planned a journey to the uninhabited territories of the west, where they hoped to find solace and peace.

As badly as the Mormons were treated, when they settled in Utah, they somehow did not pass on to the next generation any hatred or desire for vengeance for what had happened to them. Their new leader and prophet, Brigham Young, counseled them to put aside their anger and leave judgment and any retribution in the hands of God. And so they lived in relative peace, looking forward with faith that they were now safe. This was the environment my mother was born into.

When Mother lived there, the citizens of Samaria lived by a simple value system. They placed great emphasis on family, education, hard work and religion. They believed in forging strong social bonds and friendships in their community. No man was an island. Every neighbor lent a helping hand to other neighbors.

They loved celebrations in Samaria. On Pioneer Day (the twenty-fourth of July) and Independence Day, work stopped and celebrating began. The day would start with a prayer. Some of the events included very competitive horse races, games, and a rodeo in the town square. Pioneer Day commemorated the arrival of the first party of Latter-day Saints into the Salt Lake valley in 1847. Today it is a state holiday only in Utah, but many Idahoans continue to celebrate it.

At the time of her birth, Olive's father, Tom Davis, was teaching in a one-room schoolhouse in nearby Daniels, Idaho. Her mother, Vera, sought the comforting presence of her healing father, with this, her first pregnancy. Her own mother had passed away the year before during the birth of her eleventh child. Eight months later the baby also passed away.

My grandmother Vera found great comfort in the quieting presence of her father, who placed his hands on her head and blessed her that she would have a normal birth and that both mother and child would both be fine—father and daughter hanging on to faith that Vera would survive where her mother had not. They were bolstered, no doubt, by the presence of her other set of grandparents, Samuel and Mary Ann Davis.

My mother said her first memory was waking up on a big bed and finding that she was all alone. She recalled sliding off the bed backwards and running through the house looking for her mother. Finally she went to the back door and called for her. She saw her across the field by the fence, picking wild currants to make some jelly. Mother said she remembered the relief and joy she felt when her mother answered her, saying she would be there soon. At the time they lived in a small white house on a corner by a canal.

In that same white house, when she was a little older, Indians (probably of the Bannock tribe) came to the back door asking to trade for coffee. Vera, her mother, told them they did not have any coffee but offered them other items instead. When the Indians spotted little Olive, one said, "Oh, is that your little papoose?" Terrified they were going to kidnap her, she trembled behind her mother's skirts. (It is amusing that she later called all of us her little papooses.)

When Mother was not quite two years old, she slipped out of her house and wandered away out into the fields. Her parents searched everywhere in vain. Finally they solicited the entire town to help with the search. Everyone who was able began looking for the small girl. Richard Morse, barely ten years old and astride his horse, galloped down to the willows area. Not finding anything, he turned his horse into the big cornfield to search the rows. It was late August in 1926, the corn was high and green and waved softly in the breeze. After going up and down many rows, Richard finally spied the slumbering girl in one of the shady corn rows, totally unaware of the frantic search going on around her.

When my mother related this story to me many years later, I always wondered if she had just lain back in the cool of the afternoon, the sun dress her mother made covering her chubby, little legs, and fell asleep in the arms of angels—angels that seemed to be with her throughout her life. Later, when I would hoe the corn rows of our own family garden, I found myself imagining my mother curled up asleep there among the tall corn stalks.

Mother related to me two more incidents in her youth when angels seemed to be on guard. On one occasion, after a big snowfall, she climbed a hill in back of her house and decided to look over the edge and see how far the house was below her. As she got about ten feet from the edge, a very clear voice shouted, "Go back! Go back!" She was startled and actually looked around to see if someone was nearby, but there was no one. She went back down the hill and looked up where she had been. There was a huge snowdrift hanging over the hill. If she had gone farther, she would have dropped down into the drift and not be found for a long time.

"Another time (alone with my sleigh) I looked into a big culvert where a canal ran through under the road. I could see light at the other end, and I noticed it had frozen over, so I decided to crawl through it. I had gone quite a ways, when once again I heard, 'Go back! Go back!' I turned around and started back. With every step, the ice seemed to 'wave' under my feet. If it had broken, I may have drowned, and no one would have known where to find me. I was so glad to get out of there and be safe once more. Surely someone was watching over me."

After losing her daughter in the corn field, Vera thought back to a time when she herself was the object of an hours-long search in Silver City, Utah by miners and their families: "I caused a commotion in this area by wandering away from home with a little neighborhood boy. I was about four years old, and he may have been five. My mother had dressed me in a pair of overalls that day. We wandered through the sage brush. I tripped over a wire in what had been a bonfire to burn trash. I picked myself up and followed my friend. We stopped to throw rocks down an abandoned shaft which I remember well. We liked the sound of the rocks hitting the sides as they fell down the hole. We wandered along and became very tired but kept going. At last we reached the wire fence that enclosed the house of the uncle and aunt of this boy.

When we reached the place, it was getting dark. The boy crawled through the fence and opened the gate near the house. We had to walk up steps to the front door. When we knocked at the door, they were very surprised to see us. They could not believe we even found the way to their place. They had been putting their children to bed, it was so late. They put us on a couch and gave us some food. I remember a glass of milk and some cookies. I also remember my friend's uncle having a black mustache. He picked me up and began to carry me home as my friend walked beside him hanging onto his coat.

"In the meantime, back in Silver City, the miners had been called out with every available person to look for the lost children. Finally, I remember being transferred into my father's arms and when the door was opened at my Aunt Rachel Bean's home where my mother was waiting—and the big commotion when my father carried me in through that front door."

I think it is significant that the first memories my mother and grandmother had were about being lost and returned safe to their mothers' arms. Mother believed that almost everyone has fears of being lost or abandoned. She felt home and family are an integral part of our sense of security and identity. The further away we travel from it, the more we lose who we really are.

The fact that Grandma Vera lost her mother just before giving birth to my mother may have explained the unconscious zeal with which my mother protected and cared for me and my siblings. She counted every nose to make sure that we were all together whenever we left the house. She dressed us in homemade matching shirts, so that she could see us better in a crowd. We had to report when we left the house and report when we came back, and she was always waiting up for us—always.

My mother always reminisced about her mother, Vera. She was a slight, delicate woman with soft brown eyes, smooth alabaster skin, with lovely, graceful hands. She played the piano at all the town dances. She was the oldest of her siblings and was required to work very hard while growing up. Vera always smelled like sweet lavender. Her soft dark wavy hair would brush against Mother's face when she bent down to kiss or hug her as a child. Even long after her mother's death, Olive could still remember how her mother's hair smelled and felt.

Vera's father, Ben, was the elevator operator for the mines in Knightsville, Utah. Vera said that every time her mother had a baby, her father would add another small room to their little home he had built himself. They called the house, "Added Upon." She lived in fear of the emergency whistle-blowing which meant there was a cave-in at the mines. She could barely bring herself to run up there and see the bodies being brought back to the surface in her father's elevator. Mining was a hard life, and every home was touched by tragedy.

My grandfather, Tom Davis, was a large man. He towered over Vera and had big, strong hands. He was a gentle man with a quick wit and a kind heart. His eyes had a laughing twinkle in them. He loved to read, and I think that it was because of him that my mother gained her love of books. Tom was a very intelligent man, and my mother was convinced as a girl that he knew just about everything. She trusted him, because he told her that he would never lie to her, and he never did.

My mother cherished her parents, and when they were finally both gone, I would often find her in a melancholy mood. When I asked what was wrong, she would say, "I would give anything to be with them again, even for only a minute." Then she would quietly start repeating a favorite poem that she loved:

> *Backward, turn backward, O Time in your fight,*
> *Make me a child again just for tonight!*
> *Mother come back from the echoless shore,*
> *Take me again to your heart as of yore;*
> *Kiss from my forehead the furrows of care,*
> *Smooth the few silver threads out of my hair;*
> *Over my slumbers your loving watch keep,*
> *Rock me to sleep, Mother, rock me to sleep.*

After my own mother passed in 2004, I found myself going back to that poem and yearning for the comfort of my own dear angel mother.

13

OLIVE IN FRONT OF CABIN
WHERE SHE WAS BORN

OLIVE OSMOND

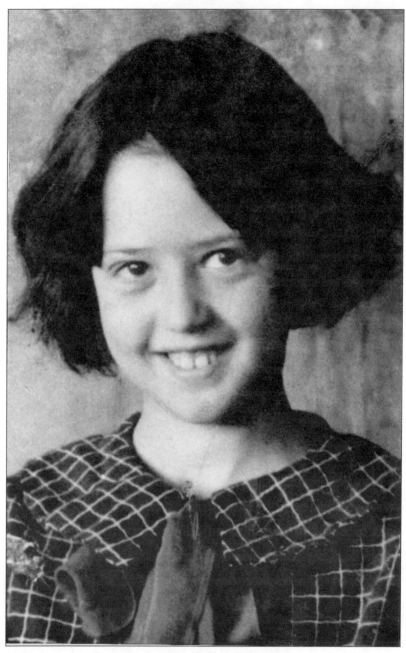

OLIVE DAVIS - AGE SIX

CHAPTER TWO

AWAKENINGS

My grandparents, Tom and Vera Davis, eventually bought a ranch about two miles above Samaria and about a mile from Tom's sister, Anna, and her family. They now had become dry farmers as well as teachers and had to plant a fixed amount from the wheat crop to meet their new mortgage payment. Up to that time, they had lived on only a teacher's salary and had rented a house. But they wanted their own place, because each year they moved from Mount Pleasant in the summer to Thatcher, Idaho in the fall where Grandpa Davis would teach for the season. (He did this for thirteen years.) Then on they would go to Logan, Utah where Grandpa himself would attend summer school. But for my mother, summers at Mount Pleasant, Idaho had always felt like home.

Today, the drive to this same newly restored farm house, which was nothing more than a three-room cabin with a shanty out back, is down a dirt road past the Samaria Cemetery and uphill two miles until one comes to a large iron gate. From this rise, where her childhood home sits, is a spectacular view of the Samaria Valley. I have been to this treasured and peaceful homestead from my mother's childhood. As I stood there on the rise looking down to the sloping valley below, the warm summer breeze wrapped around me like a soft blanket, and I felt the calm and security my mother said that she always knew there. It gives me a great deal of pleasure to think that my mother was uplifted by such a view when the family returned each summer from Thatcher.

About one hundred yards from the house sits a wooden granary, the site of what Mother called a minor miracle. Grandpa Davis had set a small fire to burn weeds in the hollow between the house and the granary. A wind blew up, and it got out of control and came roaring down the hollow where it caught the granary on fire in which the family had stored quite a bit of wheat. Grandma and my mother came running out of the house to see what they could do to help, when a truckload of men suddenly appeared with shovels in hand. They were able to quickly get control of the fire, so that it did not consume all of the family harvest. The timing of the arrival of these men was quite interesting. Unless they just "happened" to be driving by at that very moment, there was no way any one could have reached the ranch from Samaria or even from Aunt Anna's house in time.

Mother always credited it to God's hand, which she said was frequently present in her life.

My grandpa Davis was proud of his new homestead, in spite of the fact that it almost had none of the modern conveniences such as electricity or indoor plumbing, the way their rented homes had. They lived with kerosene lamps, a wood stove and water hauled from the ditch.

Grandpa put in cedar fence posts around the entire acreage—with the posts closer together than was customary. My mother remembered watching him "sighting" one post to the next, making sure they were aligned as perfectly as possible. He was so pleased with those fences. He was a hard-working man who always took the time to do things right the first time.

A ditch of water that ran in front of their house flowed down from the mountains behind them. The family used the water for bathing, washing dishes and clothes, but Mother's parents insisted they not use it for drinking purposes. Instead, they would put big milk cans wrapped in gunny sacks into the back of their car and drive down to her fraternal grandparents' house in Samaria two to three times a week. There they filled their cans from the well with what my mother described as the "coldest, best-tasting water" she ever had. They also visited and picked up their mail at the same time.

AWAKENINGS

After returning home, it was Mother's job to see that the gunny sacks around the cans were kept wet, so the wind blowing down the canyon would keep the drinking water cool. Her early experience of keeping temperatures down carried over into her married life where she struggled to keep the family at an even temperature, under some of the strenuous conditions they experienced on the road.

My mother's grandparents, Samuel and Mary Ann Davis, loved my mother and doted on her. Samuel, who had lost his hand as a young man to a threshing machine, had gone into the sheep business and was gone nearly year-round. During that time his wife, Mary Ann, opened "Aunt Mary's Shop" where she sold ice cream, cookies and candy bars to the delight of local children. They loved it when Tom and Vera brought Olive down the hill so they could spoil her and give her treats. Mother would look through the glass display case at all the jars of candy inside. Then she would walk up and down staring at the merchandise until she had picked just the right one.

The ditch of water that flowed near her house provided my mother with endless hours of pleasure. Since she had few children to play with during the months that she lived there, she learned to entertain herself by building dams and diverting the water here and there to create pools and lakes.

She had a little porcelain doll about four inches high for which she made clothes, a house, and even a luxurious little swimming hole. She got a shovel, dug a big round "pool" in part of the ditch, and waited until the muddy water settled and the pool was crystal clear. Then she created a makeshift diving board and let the doll fall off it into the water. After several dives, it hit a rock and broke off the doll's head. Mother was crushed. Money was scarce. She knew she probably would not get another one anytime soon.

These early experiences of having a life of meager means helped prepare her as a young mother, who struggled to make ends meet on our farm in North Ogden, Utah. She made all our clothes—even the boys' shirts. I remember being a little embarrassed that my brothers and I were always dressed alike. You could always pick our family out in a crowd, but I guess that was the point.

In her journals she left behind, my mother relates another use she had for the water from the ditch: "I used to make mud pies for entertainment. I sifted the soil over and over (good, black soil) until I had all the rocks and lumps out; then, I'd add water to make it just the right consistency, pour it into a variety of pans (some were bottle lids—the old metal kinds from the Mason jars) and 'baked' the cakes in the sun. I learned to unmold them at just the right time, too—when they were firm but not too dry. Then I would 'frost' them with more mud (from finely sifted dirt) and 'decorate' them with flowers (wild pink roses, yellow roses, lilacs, and a variety of wild flowers). They were lovely.

"I learned to be quite 'professional' at it. I knew exactly when they had baked long enough in the sun and got so I could turn them out without cracking them. Then I would proudly present them to my father who, bless his heart, would pretend to eat them and praise my culinary accomplishments. He always made me feel good about myself.

OLIVE – SIX YEARS OLD

Grandma Vera was ill a lot. They called it "Vera's spells." She had had appendicitis as a child, and the appendix had ruptured several times. When it was removed by Dr. Kackley in Soda Springs, Idaho, he told her it had so many scars on it from rupturing and healing over that he wondered how she had even survived. She also had several miscarriages, which compounded her ill-health. And so, for ten years before my mother's brother. Tommy, was born, Mother easily relocated from place to place and received the undivided attention of her parents.

Vera's high school days had been cut short when she was fourteen and her own mother fell ill. This required her to stay home and care for her and her siblings for some time. Even though she did not return to school, she and her sister Dora later found teaching positions in Star Valley, Wyoming. While there they boarded with my paternal grandmother LaVerna Osmond and her three small sons—one of which eventually became my mother's husband and my father!

From there Vera took a teaching job in Samaria where she met my grandfather Tom Davis, who was working on his teaching degree. After several years of corresponding, they were married December 23, 1923.

Once she became a mother, Vera turned her teaching impulses in the direction of her precocious daughter. She played the piano very well. When she got married, she inherited her father's piano and moved it to the ranch. In the evenings when chores were done, Tom and Vera would gather around the piano for some music. My mother would listen and sing along. Her favorite was "Clayton's Grand March."

It was not just Grandma Vera who played. She very patiently taught her little Olive the names of the keys, chord structures, finger exercises, how to count time and to read music. After she had learned the basics, Grandma surprised her one day with a piece of sheet music called "Moon Winks." After Mother had practiced and memorized that tune, she was rewarded with many more. I would love to have been a fly on the wall and watched my mother and grandmother as they played a waltz or show tunes together. This was the beginning of my mother's love for music; it also helped her to train my brothers to play and sing in harmony.

As I said, Mother had few friends because of the isolation of where they lived. So she invented an imaginary friend named Dora. Mother said that her friend was more than a playmate. She served as a confidante, and they had many "important" talks together for several years in her childhood.

Grandma Vera taught Mother all the practical household skills. Vera had been raised in the poverty of a mining town, so one important lesson she passed on to her daughter was not to waste anything. Every time Mother swept the floor, she had to go through the dust and remove every bobby pin and useful thing before she could throw the dirt away. Food was also never wasted. It was bottled, dried, smoked or fed to the pig or tossed in the compost pile. Every piece of material was saved and eventually became part of a quilt.

I think that this frugal living is what influenced my parents to never own a large home. We boys never did have our own bedrooms, even when my brothers became famous. We shared each other's clothes and simple living regime until we all got married and chose our own personal lifestyles. I have been married more than forty years, and my wife, Chris, and I have planted a garden and canned produce every year, as I have tried to live by my parents' example of provident living.

Grandma Vera made my mother help her can fruits and vegetables from an early age. For all the time when we were growing up, our storage shelves were lined with Mother's loving efforts—peaches, cherries, pears, tomatoes and more. Even later, when my parents and siblings were traveling all over the world, my mother was still making arrangements to buy fruit, so that she could can as soon as she got home.

Once, when Mother was a little girl, she pretended she was bottling fruit like she had seen her own mother do. She found a little bottle and packed it with lilac blossoms, covered them with water and put a cork into it. Then she placed it in her "playhouse," which was the old porch attached to the side of their house, and forgot about it. Next spring when she returned to Mount Pleasant, she was amazed to find the lilacs preserved in a kind of jelly substance.

The family traveled to Brigham City, Utah each year to buy peaches for canning. While they were there, they went into a dime store where Grandma Vera called out, "Honey, come and see these cute little bottles. Let's buy some for you, and you can help me bottle the peaches." This was the first time either of them had seen half-pint jars. Grandma Vera bought a dozen of them and had to put up with my very anxious mother, who could hardly wait to get home to start this new learning experience. When they were finished, she was so proud of all the fruit that she had canned "all by herself."

As boys, we lived on the farm in Ogden, Utah and we always helped with the apple picking so that my mother could make apple sauce and apple cider. In fact, this is how we learned to be pretty good baseball players in the process. One of us stood on a ladder—he was the pitcher. A couple of us waited on the ground with catcher's mitts. Another was the hitter. The apples were picked and sorted. Good ones were caught and tossed into baskets. The rotten ones were tossed down, pitched to the hitter who smashed them over the fence to use for fertilizer. And, being boys, we could not occasionally resist hitting the unsuspecting, grazing cows. Oh, how I loved to go down into the cellar and see those jars of apple cider!

The lessons my mother learned from Grandpa Davis were practical, and they were always embedded with philosophical nuggets. One of her memories had to do with taking lemonade to him, when he was plowing the ground with a team of horses just east of the house. He told her to watch his "pet snakes." Each time he would make a round, there would be snakes lying in the furrow. He would stop the horses, get off the plow and pet them—first with his whip and later with his glove. They just seemed to love the attention. Sure enough, next time around there they would be in the new furrow as though they were waiting for him. He told her all creatures crave and need love.

Mother remembers hunting gophers with him one day. It was early in the spring. She was having fun kicking the old tumbleweeds left from the year before, exposing all the new plants coming up that they had seeded. All at once, she kicked one and underneath it sat a great big rattlesnake, coiled up ready to strike. Her screams brought Grandpa Davis to the rescue. He grabbed his rife and blew off the snake's head. He did not say anything, but she knew that hereafter kicking tumbleweeds was not an acceptable play activity.

Once the rescue had been accomplished, Mother resumed helping with the hunt. She was pretty good at imitating the gophers and would make a high-pitched sound with her tongue *(brrrr)*, so they would stand up and Grandpa could get a good shot at them. He let her know this was not for sport. They should never take the life of any living thing, but the gophers were so numerous and eating the farmers' crops, that it was a matter of self-preservation.

One night Grandpa called her attention to a moth that was circling around the top of the lamp. He said, "Now watch that stupid moth. He just can't stay away from that fame. He will get burned sooner or later." It circled for awhile and then flew right into the center and dropped down into the fame. Grandpa likened it to temptations that would come into her life. He said, "Just don't flirt with temptations or you'll be just like that moth."

Because she was alone a lot, Mother enjoyed doing boy "stuff" with her father as much as girl activities with her mother. After hunting with her dad, she wanted her own gun. She said, "Dad bought me a cap gun and some firecrackers for the 4th of July. The smell of the cap gun going off in the car made my mother nauseated and the noise bothered her, too, so Dad told me I had to shoot it out the window or wait until I got home. When I got home I had fun with the firecrackers. I planted them in the soft mud along the ditch bank, and then put an empty can over them, ran back to the house and watched them blow the cans about as high as the trees."

But Mother certainly had her feminine side, too. She used to take a quilt out on the lawn to play with paper dolls. She not only would cut out the clothes that came with the set, but often would create and color new original designs. One day her paternal grandfather, Sam Davis, walked up from Samaria and found Mother playing on the lawn with her paper dolls. He asked if she was going to be a school teacher like her mother. She replied, "No, Grandpa, I'm going to be a dress designer." She never gave up on that idea. In fact, Mother continued to sketch dress designs throughout her life and did a great deal of sewing which planted the seed of interest in my sister, Marie, and helped lead her to create her designer doll company.

Grandma Vera decided one day that her daughter was old enough to learn how to sew. The first creation my mother made was quilt blocks sewn together in a "fan" pattern from scraps of material Grandma Vera had used for my mother's school dresses. After some practice, her mother announced, "I think it's time for you to take another step. Instead of just sewing seams, I think it would be more fun for you to make your own quilt." Mother quickly picked up this talent, and so

Grandma Vera pressed on and taught her how to put patterns together to make a dress. She had arrived!

Sewing was not as easy then as it is today with fancy sewing machines. Grandma Vera had an old treadle machine that Mother learned to use. There was no wrinkle-free material in those days either, so when things had to be ironed, Grandma Vera used the old "sad irons" (the kind that was heated on the stove top.) One Sunday they were getting ready for church. My mother had a new burgundy taffeta dress with rows of ruffles that Grandma Vera had spent hours working on. She loved that dress and had only worn it a few times. It had a few wrinkles so she decided to take it upon herself to press them out. She took the iron from the stove, not realizing it was too hot, and set it on the dress. A big bubble emerged, leaving a permanent imprint of the iron. My mother cried half the morning over the loss of that dress. Grandma Vera too was disappointed, but she took my mother's face in her hands and said, "Olive, do you think that this dress is more important to me than you are?"

Ever the extrovert, my mother loved getting letters in the mail. Some of her friends from Thatcher would write to her once in awhile, but she wanted more, so my grandma Vera bought a bunch of penny postcards and taught her how to send for free cookbooks advertised in the magazines. Then she taught her how to make indexes with the recipe titles. They would write down different categories such as cakes, cookies, and on the right side of the page would list the main ingredients. Mother found this fascinating. She collected thousands of recipes and, later in life, created three recipe books of her own. Her most popular was "The Osmond Brothers' Mother's Cookbook."

After Mother and Grandma Vera had collected, filed and indexed a number of recipe books, Grandma showed her how to plan balanced meals and create menus. Vera had always cooked for the harvesters who came to take in the wheat crop at the end of the summer. She was famous with the workers for her delicious and perfect lemon meringue pie. When Mother was about five, Vera, ever the teacher, let her help plan the meals they would serve them. In the process, she learned to be a devoted and great cook.

When we were growing up, one of her favorite dishes was 'Hunza' stew. She had read about the longevity of these Pakistani villagers and how they ate this nutrient rich stew all the time, so she created a recipe that sounded like it, and on Friday family nights we would eat homemade bread, butter, honey and that stew by candlelight in our dining room. Mother loved to set pretty tables and try new recipes. We were always her test subjects for each new dish. There were very few times we were ever disappointed.

AWAKENINGS

In a meat and potatoes state like Utah, her creative moments were really outside the box. Even my father hesitated to stick his head in the kitchen and ask her what was for dinner, because he was not sure he would understand the name of it. He would just take a whiff and, from that, he would decide if he was eating at home or making himself busy elsewhere.

When my mother was still young, she found she could send for samples that would cost from ten to twenty-five cents—items like lipstick, nail polish, face powder, and hand lotion, she jumped into that project with her usual zeal. Each Saturday when the family went shopping, she would look up her cousin, Donna, whom she also got interested in sending for samples. They would compare what they had received in the mail and exchange addresses for other items. Mother credited this time and effort as the blossoming of her love for mail order. It later helped her to learn and prepare for the day when she created and ran the highly successful Osmond Brothers Fan Club.

There were things about the ranch Mother really did not like. She was frightened when the coyotes came near around the ranch house and howled at night. Snakes made her nervous. She carried a hoe to ward them off, when she headed out into the fields to her favorite apple tree. Mosquitoes were plentiful and loved her soft skin. Since they lived close to the mountains, the thunder and lightning from summer storms were often ferocious.

And sometimes, when there was a particularly vicious storm, water would flow in torrents down the canyons toward Samaria. She related one particularly bad flood: "It had been raining quite awhile, and we were in the house. Suddenly Mother and Dad heard a strange noise—a kind of roar. They looked out just in time to see a wall of water heading toward us. Dad had just built a strong fence in front of our place with a big board gate (large enough to bring farm equipment through). When the water hit that gate which he had oiled with linseed oil, it bowed way out. We thought it would break in two, but the impact broke the force of the water and diverted it so most of it went just to the east of our house in an old hollow that had been washed out before."

When they went out to survey the damage, baby chickens that Grandma Vera was raising had been swept away. The group of chicks were all red except one little white one which had become my mother's pet. She was devastated. Then, as they walked farther to the north, Grandpa Davis noticed her little white chicken alive and up in one of the apple trees. Mother felt this was another minor miracle and gave thanks to Heavenly Father who cared about baby chicks.

AWAKENINGS

These floods often washed out the roads or made them very difficult to cross. Shortly after this storm, the family got into the car to drive down to Samaria. My mother became nervous. She began whining that her dad was going to hit one of the ditches and turn the car over. After several assurances to the contrary, Grandpa just stopped the car and let her out, so she could walk across the dip on her own. As soon as the car maneuvered through it, Grandpa stepped on the gas and took off without her (one of those teaching moments). She panicked and ran as fast as she could to catch up. As she told the story: "I had the wits scared out of me. I imagined there were snakes everywhere, and I didn't like the feeling of being alone. They stopped the car a little ways down the road and let me catch up. That cured me from ever complaining too much again."

Despite these inevitable encounters with Nature, perhaps the best summation of her early life on Mount Pleasant came from something Mother wrote in her journal dated: "Summer, 1930: Dad sold the horses and bought a tractor for the ranch. I loved to ride on it with him. I would sit on the fender that covered the big wheel and hang on to the exhaust pipe that went up. He would only allow me to ride when he was on straight ground. He said it was too dangerous when he would plow around the hills. I loved to watch the seagulls following us and picking up worms. Everything seemed to be so calm and peaceful. When we were in Mount Pleasant, there was never a care in the world."

OLIVE – SEVEN YEARS OLD

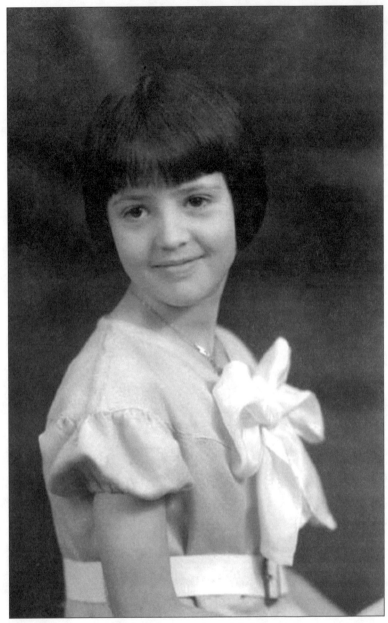

OLIVE - AGE EIGHT

CHAPTER THREE

DISCOVERING

My mother's first memory of Thatcher, Idaho was when she was about three years old. The highway department was repairing the roads, and the big trucks and equipment would go back and forth in front of their rented house. Her parents worried that she would slip out of the house and into the road, so they repeatedly warned her about the dangers lurking outside. With the clear rationale of a three year old, she retorted one day, "Well, if they run over me, it will be their fault."

At that time the family lived in a little two-room log cabin. They cooked and heated the house with a coal stove. For a closet in the bedroom, they hung a big curtain at the end of the room. Besides clothes, they kept food supplies—canned goods, a sack of sugar, a sack of four, and other sundries. Tom and Vera's bed barely ft into the room. Olive's little black iron bed was squeezed in right beside it, so someone had to crawl over one bed to get to another. Both beds had squeaky springs, and sometimes Mother would jump from one to the other just to hear them squeak. She said that she imagined the sound they made was like little birds chirping. When she became frightened at night, she sought the comfort of her father's strong hand and held onto it until she could go back to sleep. To make sure he stayed awake to watch over her, she would pat his hand gently until she drifted off. Some nights he would awake and find her patting his hand in her sleep.

The other room in their cabin served as a kitchen. An old wooden cupboard served as her mother's pie safe. It had two tin doors that had tiny holes punched in them in the design of stars. When Grandma Vera made a pie, she would place it in there to cool. My mother loved to sit by the doors and take in the sweet goodness that wafted through the room. There were also shelves that hung on the wall where Vera kept her blue pottery plates and cast iron pans.

The room contained a coal stove, a small daybed, and a couple of chairs. The walls were painted a faded green. Around the room ran a three-inch band of painted, white molding which circled around the middle of the walls, dividing top from bottom. Mother remembered her father would use space in the molding to hold sheet music, so he could practice his trombone.

The house was "banked" around the foundation with sand about two feet deep and two feet high. It was a perfect sand box where Mother made roads and castles while playing with her imaginary friend Dora and creating fantasy worlds to her heart's content. The back yard sloped up to a big canal, and in the spring, when the snow melted, the water ran down to the house.

As in Samaria, Mother had both dirt and water to play in along with a Christmas present she got that consisted of small cooking utensils. There was a tiny egg beater, pancake turner, and a big variety of aluminum pans. Nothing gave her more pleasure or occupied more of her time as her cooking toys.

There was a neighbor a few yards from this home in Thatcher who had three children. That was a treat compared to Mother's isolation in Samaria. The children's names were Ruth, Helen and Grant. In the fall, Mother and Helen loved to rake up leaves and pile them into "houses" and burrow out a number of different rooms. Then they collected empty cans and bottles for their imaginary food supplies. Mother said that there was something mystical about covering herself in the leaves and hiding away. She loved the sound of them, as they crunched and crackled beneath her, and the patterns that they made as they lay above her. Though the fall air was cool, she felt warm and safe within them. While she lay there silently listening to the breeze moving the leaves above her, she would let her mind wander or sing to herself.

DISCOVERING

One evening Vera and Tom took Olive on a visit to the neighbors' home. While the parents talked in the living room, Mother's friend, Grant, suggested the kids should make a slide in the kitchen, and my mother decided she knew just how to do it. She mixed four, sugar, salt and pepper together and spread it across the floor. They had a wonderful time taking turns sliding across the room. Eventually, Grandpa Tom began hearing something banging against one wall and then against another, accompanied with a lot of giggling. He opened the kitchen door and discovered their game.

Needless to say, they had a lot of cleaning up to do. This same house was the scene of Mother's first major childhood accident. She was there, playing "Run Sheep Run" with her three friends. They were chasing each other around the outside of the house at top speed. As Olive soared off their front porch, she fell onto a big, green planter and broke her elbow in three places. Her friends' mother tried to help her, but she sat crying and would not move until her father came to get her.

Since Thatcher had no medical facilities, her parents had to take her to the hospital in Soda Springs to have it set. Mother remembered holding her arm close to her chest during the bumpy ride to the hospital while her mother cradled her in her lap. The only thing that she remembered about the hospital was laughing at the sound of gurgling water going down a drain somewhere in the emergency room. She said that she was only afraid until she had her father's hand to hold.

It was in their little cabin in Thatcher that my mother began to wonder about the miracles of life and nature. Once she found a dead bird in the yard. She sat quietly as she stared at it for a long time, first touching its still warm wings, then looking into its lifeless eyes. *Why do things have to die?* she wondered. *And why do we get to live?*

She took a spoon and dug a grave for the bird. Then she placed grass at the bottom of the hole and flowers at one end for a pillow. She remembered she rolled the bird with her spoon into the grave and positioned its head on the flowers. Then she covered it with more grass and some dirt. She dropped pebbles in a circle around the grave and stuck a flower in the middle. Only after completing this ritual did she go back to playing. In later years, she questioned why she remembered this event in such detail.

Once, after visiting friends in Thatcher on a cold fall night, she and her parents arrived home to a cabin that was quite cold. Grandpa Tom built a fire, and they decided to go to bed right after supper to keep warm. Grandma Vera warmed up mashed potatoes with some canned milk, salt and pepper. Mother remembered how delicious that simple meal tasted and how secure she felt snuggling into her little bed with her parents right next to her side.

Grandma Vera used to smile at her precocious daughter's love for pencils, papers and books. My mother loved to organize even at this early age. She would organize her toys or precisely line up her mother's spices in the cupboard. Sometimes she would choose to do it alphabetically: allspice, cinnamon, nutmeg, oregano—or by size or color of the cans. She once organized her father's books by size, which caused quite a stir since he had them shelved according to subject. But he was good-natured about it. Mother felt that any job went better if it was organized right. She was so convinced of this she later in life wrote a small book called, "Let's Get Organized," which sold quite well in the 1970's.

Mother was reading long before she started school. Her father brought home a workbook with pictures one could color and paste onto another sheet. Mother remembered how pleased he was when she could read to him what was on each paper: "The little girl ran to the door and saw a big frog on the floor." She colored the girl and frog, cut them out and pasted them into the proper place. He decided then and there that she could read so well, she should start school right away. But instead of putting her in first grade, he registered her in the second grade because he thought she would be bored doing first grade work.

The school in which my mother attended and my grandfather taught in was nothing more than a two room cabin. Grades one through four were in my mother's classroom, which the children called the "little room." And the one where Grandpa Tom taught grades five through eight was called the "big room." On the porch of the school was an old ship's bell used to call the children in after recess. There was no bathroom, only an outhouse with a pail of lye and a small shovel for dumping into the hole when a child was done. They got their water from a well.

There was no play equipment. The boys played marbles or ball, and the girls skipped rope or sat around sharing stories. During winter weather months, the children would draw, sing or do art projects inside.

"My first school teacher was Josephine Roghaar, and we all loved her dearly. When we would go outside for recess, we each wanted to hold her hand, so she took turns walking around the school grounds with one child on each side.

"She made each of us feel important. She always had some project for us to do besides our 'reading, writing and arithmetic.' For example, she set up a big sand table on one side of the room where we could play when it was too cold outside. One day she brought in little trees and little figures of ice skaters, and we made an ice skating pond with blue paper and cotton. When our parents came for PTA night, we were delighted to show them our handiwork."

Because my mother was able to spend so much time with her parents every day, they had a very special bond with each other. Because they were so close, my mother felt comfortable sharing her innermost feelings with them and asking those deep questions which were running around in her head. Grandma Vera was her source for all things domestic and musical. But with Grandpa Tom, she would share her deepest thoughts and ask her most pressing questions. She would curl up in his lap and pat his hands as they talked. Her most treasured moments were when she would have him explain a scripture that he was reading. This always led to more questions about where she came from and why she was on earth; where people went when they died; why bad things happened; why do we laugh and cry?

In those early years, she did not remember all that he told her, but she recalled when she would finally slip out of his lap after a talk, her world felt safe and her mind calm.

My mother liked to rough house and play hard physically. One memory she left in her journal illustrates this: "In the winter we all brought our sleighs to school and would go out at noon recess and ride down the little hills close by. I was at the top of one of these hills just east of the school house when I heard the bell ring and started down the hill going pretty fast. A little boy walked right in front of me and I could not help running into him. My sleigh caught him right at knee level and made him sit down on the front of it, and I took him right up to the school house steps. I don't know why that struck me so funny, but to this day I have to laugh when I think about it. He was so totally unaware of what had happened and just sat there dazed on my sled."

Those early elementary school years were spent traveling between Thatcher and Mount Pleasant—a ninety-mile journey. Although my mother became more and more invested in people and happenings in Thatcher as time went on, extended family members back in Samaria played an important role in her perception of who she was. Grandma Vera came to dislike Mount Pleasant, because she felt lonely and isolated from her neighbors. As a result, they made several trips to Samaria each week to visit her grandparent's cabin.

Many of Olive's memories surround the warmth and love she experienced in that three-room home. She wrote in her journal: "When we moved back to the ranch from Thatcher each spring, Grandma Mary would always wait up for us no matter how late. As soon as we got near to their house, we could see the light twinkling on their porch, and Dad would always say, "Bless her heart. She is up waiting for us." That light on the porch had a profound effect on my mother. It felt like a warmth in her heart that told her all was well—that here was a place of safety.

My mother loved her grandparents. They were soft-spoken, gentle country folk. They had strong religious convictions, a hard work ethic and simple needs. They were so content with so little. When my mother would ask them why they did not want or have more, they always found her question curious. "Why?" her grandpa would ask. "We sort of like things just as they are. No need for more. More complicates life."

How strange, Mother thought. Yet, after my brothers and Marie had become famous, and my mother and father had traveled with them around the world, and after their nest emptied, where did my parents go? They moved to a little house in the small rural town of Ephraim, Utah. There they had a small garden and lived a very simple life.

One day I asked my mother, "Why did you happen to move here?"

Her answer echoed the wisdom of her grand-father, "We have no need for anything bigger. Life gets too complicated when you have too much."

Mother liked going down to her grandparents' house. She once said that her grandmother was a "good fixer." And she was. She knew how to cook and bake the best meals and breads. And the "good fixer" title stayed in the family a long time. There was never a time when Great-grandma Mary Davis did not have food ready for the family. Whenever they sat down to the table, she always put a little ice cream spoon at my mother's place. That was called "Olive's spoon." Mother would look for it at the table, so she would know where she was supposed to sit. This spoon had once been part of Mary's little candy store where she served her home-made ice cream, lemonade, and cookies.

Mother's paternal grandfather, Sam Davis, always got up early in the morning and built a fire in the stove, so the house would be warm when everyone else woke up. When my mother stayed there, she would slip off their old horsehair couch where she slept and rise early with him. He would make her a little cup of hot cocoa and pull a chair close up to the warm stove. Then he would put her in his lap where she would sip from her cup, while he read his scriptures.

DISCOVERING

One of the other comforts that she enjoyed when she stayed with her grandparents was an old Regulator clock that hung on the wall. At night, when she lay on the couch, the clock would tick softly like a mother's heartbeat. She wrote that there was something peaceful and reassuring about that clock. She said it sounded like it was the heart of the world; and, as long as it kept ticking, she was sure that all would be well.

Mother liked to go out to the barn with her grandfather to feed the pigs and chickens. He would mix up a big bucket of bran for the pigs which she got to stir. He also let her throw grain to the chickens, to her delight. It made her laugh at the way they pecked and scratched. Every once in awhile, Grandpa chopped off a chicken's head, so the family could eat the chicken. My mother was there once when he did it. She stood in shock as the chicken jumped around headless. She was so traumatized, she would not eat chicken for a long time.

No one ever got away from her grandparent's house without at least having a piece of cake. Mary always had a special boiled raisin cake with powdered sugar frosting ready when anyone came. She kept it in her little pie safe with her spices and other baking supplies. Mother loved to open the doors just to get a whiff of the wonderful aromas coming from the goodies in there.

Speaking of aromas, in the hallway by the back door, Grandma Mary had a wash stand with a pitcher full of water, a small basin and a bar of lemon soap. Mother washed her hands many times whenever she went there, so they would smell like lemons. Years later, she searched and searched for lemon soap that smelled the same, but she was never able to find any.

The grandparents' walls in their living room and bedroom were the "whitest white" my mother had ever seen. These were covered with large pictures of relatives in old ornate frames. Her grandfather used to name each one and tell her stories about them and where they came from. It fascinated her when he said, "They are part of you and who you are. Always remember them." I am certain this was the beginning of my mother's love and interest in genealogy.

Another item that Mother loved was their big, old coal stove. It had warming ovens on the top and large water reservoirs to the side to heat the water for washing dishes or bathing.

One day her grandparents were making ice cream out in the back of the cabin for a family party. My mother put a piece of ice in her mouth and before she realized it, it had slipped down and lodged in her throat. She could not swallow and could not get her breath. She was terrified. She ran into the house and got her mother's attention. Grandma Vera took one look at her, tipped her upside down and beat on her back. "The ice came out and I gasped a deep breath!" she wrote. "I've thought about that incident many times over the years— how my mother knew instantly what to do. I thought she was the most amazing person in the world—she saved my life."

Music was a medium of expression for this extended family, even for little Olive. Her grandfather kept a small organ at the foot of the couch on which she learned to play "Two Little Hands." It was very hard to reach the pedals and pump them with her feet. But, to the delight of her grandfather, she figured out how to hang right off the little bench just so she could work them with her toes.

When she was not playing the organ, she was playing her grandfather's old wind-up phonograph machine. This instrument fascinated her. A hard disk sat inside on a spinning circle. There was a little arm on the side of the disk which had a needle in it, and when the needle touched the disk, music came through the speaker on the side. The voices and music sounded a little scratchy and distorted, but to her it was a miracle. She spent hours putting on the records, winding it up and singing or humming along, while she stood on a chair to reach the "winder."

Mother remembered one night when some local men came over to practice with her grandfather for a men's quartet. Vera played the piano while Grandpa Ben Nichols sang and played the violin. They sang, "Just A Song at Twilight." She loved the harmony. It was the first time that she had ever heard barbershop singing. She marveled at the way their voices blended and rose and fell with each note. She said that her whole body began to tremble with excitement, and later she begged her grandfather to teach it to her. So he taught her a little melody, and then he would sing the harmony to it. Little did she realize just how much barbershop would become a part of her future.

One final memory Mother had of her time with her paternal grandparents was when she stayed down at their cabin while her parents attended the Mormon temple in Logan, Utah. "Night came, and I got pretty lonesome. I heard those darn dogs barking off in the distance, and they made me scared. I did not like being away from my parents, so I began to cry. Grandma took me in her arms and sat me in her lap and rocked me in her old rocking chair, which had been in the family for a long time. The wood stain was worn off where Grandma's hands rested on the arms. Every time she rocked, it creaked like cracking wood. "I must have gone to sleep, because that's the last thing I heard until my parents got home."

DISCOVERING

OLIVE WITH TOMMY

OLIVE, FATHER AND TOMMY

OLIVE DAVIS – THIRD GRADE BAND
(Olive third from left, top row. Tom Davis, top middle)

TOM DAVIS' CLASS – OLIVE, CENTER FRONT

CHAPTER FOUR

SHARING

Vera's father, Benjamin Nichols, was a remarkable man. He was a hard worker. His hands were calloused and worn from toil, and his face leathered and drawn from hardship. All that he did, his whole focus, was for his wife and eleven children. He built his own house in the mining town of Knightsville, where he was honored and trusted by the community. Though life was hard for him, he was a happy man and found joy in his family and in the simple things of life.

One day he surprised his wife by buying the first copper tub in town. They had no plumbing, so they still had to fill it up with buckets of water. He put a hole in the floor to drain it under the house and dug a ditch for the water to flow out into the street. That tub was the talk of the town for quite awhile.

Grandma Vera remembered he would make every one of his children take baths on Saturday, so they would all be clean for Sunday church. When the water drained down the street after the baths were over, neighbors would see the bubbles flowing by and say, "Well, I guess the Nichols will be in church tomorrow!" This would embarrass Vera so much she would go outside and stir the bubbles up into the mud with a stick, hoping no one would know who the water belonged to.

Ben Nichols was also a religious man. Each morning he would wake his family by playing the hymn, "Welcome, Welcome Sabbath Morning," on their piano in the parlor. He would make sure all his children sat reverently in church, too. He was honest and always paid his debts quickly and never borrowed anything that he could not bring back in better condition than before he got it.

Mother told me that the joy went out of him after his wife died. She said he became lonely and lost. He loved and depended so much on his beloved wife. He had worked in the mines most of his life, but after her death, he felt he should take his family away from the mines and get a little farm. So he bought a few acres in Payson, Utah. After Vera got married and moved to Samaria, Idaho, she took three of her little brothers to raise. Soon her father bought a home in Samaria, and some of Vera's siblings continued to live nearby.

My mother was surrounded and lovingly influenced by these many extended members of her family. Among them was this grandfather and Aunt Helen and Uncle Willard. She wrote about Willard numerous times in her journal: "Willard was just seven years older than I was and he was fun to be around. He had a darling smile and pretty teeth. He could whistle like no one else I had ever heard—and he was always whistling! I remember how 'brave' I once thought he was for opening a trap door in the kitchen and going down in the dark pit of the root cellar for some potatoes and carrots they had stored there." Just about everyone had root cellars for their winter vegetable storage, but my mother did not like them. They were cold and dark, and she was sure that they were full of bugs.

Sometimes, when Mother was visiting Willard, they would get a sweet tooth and sneak into the kitchen to beat egg whites very stiff with sugar and vanilla. Then they would sit under the kitchen table and eat their "candy" by the spoonful. Vera was not happy that they had wasted egg yokes to do this and always scolded them and made them do an extra chore to pay for it.

It was Willard's job to milk the cow and separate the cream. My mother was fascinated as she watched him pour a bucket of milk in the top of the separator and see the cream squirt out one spout and the separated milk out the other. She then helped the family churn cream into butter and gave the other milk to pigs and chickens. Churning was hard work, and her arms grew tired very quickly. When it was done, Vera would put the butter into a crock. She loved the butter with her mother's homemade wheat bread.

She also remembered a time when Willard pitched a tent just outside the house. Olive asked him if she could gather her paper dolls together and play with them inside. He said it was okay, but a few minutes after she got settled, it started to rain. She recalled how wonderful it smelled as it hit the dry, parched ground. She loved listening to the thumping of the raindrops on the tent roof as it fell faster and faster. She felt cozy, warm and dry in her little shelter.

"The intoxicating smell of the wet, new-mown hay from the adjacent fields filled my lungs. The only jarring elements were the thunder and lightning that ripped through the surrounding hills and made me nervous. Then, as suddenly as it had begun, it slowed and stopped. The clouds parted and the sun created a beautiful rainbow against the mountain where it was still raining. I followed the rainbow shape with my finger and counted all the colors. Then I lay down in the door of the tent and watched as water dripped from the roof—now and again catching a drop with my finger."

My mother thought Aunt Helen was an amazing girl. "I loved to watch her work. She kept the house so neat and clean and made such delicious meals. She baked bread every week, and it was so good. I remember how she always washed her hands and cleaned under her fingernails before she would knead it. She was quite young too, and yet had so many responsibilities in the family. When my grandma Olive Booth Nicholes died, it took everyone working together to fill her place. One does not realize how much a mother does until she is not there to do it."

Her aunt was a teenager whom Mother followed around and always tried to imitate. "She was so good to me. Whenever we went there, she would take time to talk to me about all the silly girl things in my head. She had lots of friends and would often go to the dances in Malad. I could not wait for the time when I grew up and could do the same things."

She recalled that Helen had such pretty wavy hair, and she would set it with a special kind of setting solution she made herself from boiled flaxseed.

Aunt Helen's Wave Setting Solution

Boil together 3 cups water–1 cup flaxseed (whole or ground)
Cool until a jelly is formed. Strain to remove seeds.
Apply to hair after shampoo.

"I don't know how good that smelled, but apparently it worked," she wrote.

Not all relatives were loving and supportive. Once, relatives from California came to visit Grandpa Nichols' family. Among the group was a boy my mother's age whom she had never met. They were in the kitchen, getting acquainted, when he asked if she was thirsty. She replied in the affirmative, so he put a dipper into a bucket of drinking water. Instead of pouring the water into a glass, he threw the dipper of water all over her. She thought he was the meanest boy she had ever met.

When Mother was eight years old, she was baptized by immersion into the Church of Jesus Christ of Latter-day Saints (The Mormons). In the Latter-day Saint belief, children are first blessed as an infant and given a name which is recorded on the rolls of the church, but they do not become a member of the church until they are eight and have reached what is called the "age of accountability," when it is believed they then know the difference between right and wrong.

In her journal, my mother recalls: "I believe there were five or six of us baptized that day. As I remember, we were all wearing overalls and were baptized in Portage Ditch by my father who held the Melchizedek Priesthood and had the authority to do so. Since he did the baptizing and I was his daughter, he said I should go first. (We were all a bit frightened, and I don't believe any of us kids knew how to swim at the time.) The water was quite deep and very cold from the spring runoff. I didn't remember to hold my nose when I went under the water, and it seemed like I swallowed half the ditch. I thought for sure I would drown."

The night before Mother was baptized was very special for her. She told me she had an "interview" with her father where they talked about baptism. He asked her how she felt about being baptized, and if she felt worthy. She said she did. He then explained the covenant of baptism she was making with the Lord. "In the covenant, you take upon you the name of Christ and become a Christian. You agree to keep Heavenly Father's commandments, to help and comfort others and serve the Lord."

"In return," he explained, "the sacrificing atonement of the Lord becomes active in your life. He gives you the gift of repentance, so when you make mistakes, you can come to Him and ask for forgiveness, and He will do so." My mother reached for his large hand and looked into his face with adoring eyes.

"He also gives you the gift of the Holy Ghost to guide and direct you and help you to tell the difference between right and wrong. When you come out of the waters of baptism, you will be clean and pure before the Lord," Grandpa told her.

After Mother came out of the water in the ditch, she said she felt the mud squishing between her toes, and she was cold. But she said there was just this little feeling inside of her that seemed to say, "This is right."

The following Sunday, she was presented to her ward (the local church congregation) to be welcomed as a new member. Then she sat in a chair while her father and a couple other priesthood holders placed their hands on her head and conferred upon her the Gift of the Holy Ghost. After the men removed their hands from her head, she said that she waited to see if she felt its presence. She was not sure what it would feel like. Her father explained that the Holy Ghost is a gift to be cultivated, and a companion to be treasured. It worked upon the principle of, "Knock, and the door shall be opened; seek and ye shall find."

Mother wrote that she felt her life change after she was baptized. She felt more mature and more responsible. She loved the Savior and the lessons about His life and teachings that she read in both the Bible and the Book of Mormon. Her family met each morning and evening for prayer and scripture reading. She loved the way her father explained spiritual principles. She said they gave her great hope and comfort. And she loved the prophet of the church, who at that time was Heber J. Grant. She said she felt safe knowing he spoke for the Savior, and by following him, she was following what He wanted for her.

The next school year, the family moved to another log house in Thatcher across the street from the grade school. Tom purchased a phonograph machine for the family, partly because Mother loved her grandfather's machine so much. She remembered one of the songs on a children's records which went like this:

What a lot of things to see
On the way to school
Squirrels running up a tree
On the way to school
Sparrows building cunning nests
Robins smoothing down their vests
What a lot of things to see—on the way to school.

(I am amazed at my mother's memory. I can't remember as many details of my early life as she did.)

Vera, as I said, was an excellent cook. Being the oldest girl in a family of eleven and having a mother who was an excellent cook herself helped, I am sure. In fact, Vera's own grandmother once had a boarding house and used to cook for many boarders.

SHARING

Olive used to watch closely when her mother cooked. She would give her a lot of tips. "Don't handle the pastry dough any more than you have to." "Cook meat at a low temperature—high temperatures make it tough." "Tear the lettuce rather than cutting it." Vera made wonderful cookies, and Olive enjoyed eating the dough as much as the baked ones. "I remember getting caught taking a spoonful behind her back. Ha!"

In May 1935, the family dynamics shifted dramatically. Vera was a frail woman and had difficulty carrying a pregnancy through to term. She had many miscarriages after her daughter's birth. Finally, Vera became pregnant again. The doctor told her to go to bed and stay there if she ever wanted to carry this baby to full term. So she did as she was told, and my mother had to take on extra responsibilities for the next few months.

Mother had been an only child all these years. She wondered how it would be to now share her home, her life and her parents with a sibling. She imagined all the fun scenarios of having a little sister and then would realize she might have a brother, so she rehearse that possibility. But mostly she worried about how her parents would be able to love her as much when they had a new child. Would they wind up loving it more than her?

My grandfather Tom told me that one day, as it came close to the birth, Mother crawled into his lap as she always did when she had something important to talk to him about. She fidgeted for awhile, and then asked, "Daddy, how much do you love me?"

Tom paused for a moment to understand the point of the question and then answered, "A whole lot."

"Will you love me as much as the new baby?" she asked.

His answer settled any doubts she had. "Every child that comes into a home brings with it a special gift that makes every mother and father's love grow even more, so they can love everybody the same." That was all she needed to know.

So Mother was unseated as the only child, when her brother Tommy was born in Thatcher. She wrote that she was very excited by his arrival. She was ten by then and saw her brother more as her child than a rival for her parents' affections.

Some of her mother's friends had a baby shower before his birth. Olive remembered the lovely smell of the Johnson's baby powder they brought. And then there was that special gift—a little delicate jacket made of aqua-blue Japanese silk, embroidered with little flowers. She thought was the prettiest thing she had ever seen.

The first of May, a nurse named Mrs. Condie, moved in with the family for a few days, and then a doctor was called in when the birth became imminent. Mother had never been around someone who had given birth before. As things progressed and people were scurrying about, she felt suddenly scared so she stepped outside on the porch and said a little prayer. Shortly after, Tommy was born, whole and hearty. Mother recalled her father's expression of joy and happiness that he finally had a son. "Tommy had lots of black hair, and he was so cute. I had never been around a baby before, so it was really exciting for me. I could not leave him alone. He missed being born on my birthday by one day. His was May 3 and mine May 4."

"Shortly after Tommy was born," Olive wrote, "school was out and we moved back to the ranch for the summer. It was a hectic move. Tommy cried a good deal of the time, and Mother was distraught and exhausted wondering what to do for him. They took him to the doctor several times, but he could find nothing wrong. Finally one visit, he suggested that Tommy might just be hungry and should be given formula for a supplement in addition to breast feeding. That solved the high-pitched wailing, and everyone finally got some peace! He really took to the bottle, which he continued using until he was almost two.

"As time went on, Tommy got teeth and chewed on the nipple. He finally bit right through it and it became useless. But he would not drink his formula out of a glass. So my father went down to the little store in Samaria to get a new nipple for Tommy's bottle, but all they had were big, black nipples for feeding lambs that could be secured to the top of a pop bottle. So he brought one home and fixed it up for Tommy. He took to it like a duck takes to water. But he could not understand why we made him leave it home when we went somewhere, but we did not want anyone to see it. It was really laughable."

That same summer, Mother caught whooping cough and had to stay away from her little brother. There are vaccinations for the disease today, but back in 1935, there was none. It is a highly contagious bacterial disease that causes uncontrollable, violent coughing. This coughing can make it very hard to breathe. A deep "whooping" sound is often heard when an infected individual tries to inhale. It usually last about six weeks and can be fatal if an infant contracts it.

"What a disappointment that was," Mother recalled. "I loved him so much and wanted to hold him and play with him but as long as I had this 'barking'

cough (which was a long time), I couldn't go near him."
He was kept in the north part of their little house and
she had to stay in the south end.

As soon as she recovered, she became like a
second mother to Tommy. She helped him learn to crawl
and walk. She also became aware of the big difference in
parenting boys and girls. He was so much louder than
she was and so much more aggressive—getting into
everything and throwing things around.

One day she found him, hanging on the screen
door and kicking their baby kittens off the porch one by
one. She was really upset at first but kept her feelings
hidden. He was, after all, a boy, she told herself. Tommy
was the perfect subject for Mother to work on, to prepare
her for becoming the mother of eight boys!

My mother was always surrounded by music.
Each year, the school had a Christmas play, and Vera
played the piano while each child had a chance to
perform. Tom would direct, and parents, grandparents
and friends would come from all over the valley to see
the production.

One day, her father arranged for a high school
music teacher to come to the grade school once a week,
give music lessons and start a little band. Tom had
taught a young student in school who had learned to
play the saxophone really well.

One night he said to his daughter, "The Wrights have invited us to come to their place and hear Fern play the saxophone."

Mother recalled: "What a motivation that was for me—which was just what Dad had hoped for! Fern played a tune called 'Saxophobia,' and I immediately wanted to learn to play the saxophone—and especially to play that 'Saxophobia' music. I expressed my desire to the music teacher. He laughed and suggested that maybe I should learn 'Yankee Doodle' first."

Her father bought his young Olive a used C melody saxophone at first. He wanted to make sure she liked playing a saxophone before he invested in an E-fat Alto like Fern had. She practiced diligently every day, and soon her lips were in shape. She could get some pretty good sounds from that old saxophone. It helped that Vera had already taught her to read notes and play the piano fairly well. It also helped that Vera was a very patient person and that Tommy giggled and got excited when she played.

"Yankee Doodle" was the first song that she learned from a little booklet the music teacher gave her, but that just whetted her whistle. She was on to more difficult pieces and loved every minute of it. "Saxophobia" was still her goal. Finally, she saved up enough money from her own allowance and went to the music store to buy it. She practiced and practiced until she was able to play it—although not perfectly because it was a difficult piece. Some time later she was able to master it well enough to play it in public. She continued to play and love the saxophone for many years and when the time came, all her sons learned to play it from her instructions.

My mother started the eighth grade when she was twelve. The family, rented a part of the "Bevans' House" about a mile from the school in her seventh grade year and then moved back across the street from the school in her eighth year. In the winter she and her friend, Margaret White, were assigned to sort some books in the library at school. She had torn the pocket on her dress while playing outside at recess and had pinned it back with a straight pin she borrowed from the teacher. The library was cold. The two were wearing their coats. Mother said aloud, "Wow, it's cold in here!" and squeezed both hands into her coat pockets. That straight pin came right through her coat and pierced her right hand just below the joint of her middle finger.

As she recalled: "It really hurt, but that wasn't the worst of it. That night I developed a fever and my hand started swelling. I was feeling so miserable the next morning I could not go to school. By evening, I could not stand to even touch my hand, and my fever was climbing. We soaked the hand in hot water, but my parents decided I needed a doctor so they took me to Grace, Idaho and we got the doctor out of bed. He decided to lance it. He poured some alcohol on my hand and then slashed it open with a sharp knife. I thought I was going to faint. Hurt? Yes, indeed."

They returned home, but Mother's hand got worse, so her parents called Mrs. Condie, the same nurse that attended Tommy's birth. She lived a few miles away and came over to help take care of my mother. She soaked the finger and put poultices on it. But after a short time, she suggested that Mother be taken back to the hospital.

Dr. Kackley was the doctor. He took one look and rushed her into surgery. She remembered how frightened she was when they put the mask on her face to administered ether. True to form, her father stayed right there with her, undoubtedly holding her hand.

Mother's hand was so swollen by this time that the doctor had to cut into it over an inch deep with the surgical knife. There was a lot of drainage. Since there were no antibiotics to kill the infection, they wrapped her hand with bandages about three or four inches thick all around, poured water over it and put her hand in a little electric oven to bake. Occasionally the nurses came in and poured more water over it. My mother's heart was nearly broken when they took the bandages off, and the tendon in her finger had shrunk, so much that she could not straighten out her finger. She cried and cried, because she was afraid she would not be able to play her saxophone any more. But she taught herself to play again—even though that crooked finger was a "thorn in her flesh" throughout the rest of her life.

Olive and her father shared a dual role—daughter and father, student and teacher. She thought Tom was the best father and teacher in the world. She recalled that he had a philosophy about teaching. He believed a teacher should be "Fair, Firm and Friendly," and he said, "If the student hasn't learned, the teacher has not taught."

"He put his heart and soul into his teaching and gave special attention to students during lunch time, at recess, after school or other special times, and to anyone that was having trouble keeping up with their lessons. He taught English so well. In teacher's college he had learned from his professor that 'You must learn the rules and then learn to apply the rules.' He taught us the same way. He put them on the blackboard along with examples and drilled us day after day, year after year. There were four grades in his room—fifth, sixth, seventh, eighth. Things such as grammar rules, spelling words, etc. were constantly being put on the blackboard, so we could easily memorize them."

"Even though there were four grades in the same room, he took one grade at a time and, using different text books, he taught different lessons. As I look back, I can see why the eighth grade was so easy. By the time we had gone through the four different grades, we had pretty well learned what the eighth graders needed to know to pass the standard exams."

Tom wanted all of his students to be achievers, and he would try to motivate them with stories about great people to inspire them. He hung pictures of George Washington and Abraham Lincoln on the walls, and he would often quote from great writers like Emerson and Voltaire.

Each Friday he sponsored a spelling bee. All the grades stood up around the room, and Tom would give each one a word to spell. If they spelled the word right, they kept standing. If they missed, they took their seats. Mother remembered being next to the last one day and went down on the word, "wrestle." Her father had pronounced it, "rassle." But she was always one of the best spellers in school.

"I usually got good grades on my tests," Mother wrote, "and some of the other kids would say, 'You have an advantage, because your dad is the teacher.' But I can honestly say that he did not show any favoritism at all.

He made me work just as hard for my grades as any other student.

"In fact, to show how concerned he was for the feelings of others, here's a little story: He kept the scores in a notebook of each of our Friday tests. Those averaged scores were kept in another part of his notebook and, in the spring of the year, when it was time for the eighth grade to graduate into high school, those scores were also averaged, and the one with the highest score was honored as the valedictorian for the year.

"The year that I graduated my score happened to be the highest. He showed it to me in his notebook and then he said, 'Honey, you and I both know it, but it creates a real problem for me. We don't want anyone's feelings to get hurt, do we? And besides, some of the student's parents are on the school board, and I surely would not want them to think I was favoring my own daughter. So, if you do not mind too much, I think it would be best if we do not have a valedictorian this year. Is that all right with you?'

"I was a little disappointed, but I understood and it was all right with me. Anything my Dad did I knew was fair and right. I loved him so much! I had even more respect for my wonderful Dad for being so thoughtful."

Another memory from that classroom Mother remembered: "I always had to laugh when things were funny, and if it wasn't appropriate to laugh, I tried to hold it back, but then tears would run down my cheeks trying to squelch it. One day my friend, Margaret, and I were sitting together reading current events in class. Everyone would take turns reading something from these little weekly papers. Margaret rolled her copy up into a roll and blew on it. It made a funny squeak that surprised us, and we both started to laugh. We absolutely couldn't stop, which, of course, disturbed everyone else.

Dad looked at us and said sternly, "You two may exit to the hall and stay there until you can come back and act like ladies! But we still could not keep from laughing. We had a good laugh outside, but in a little while we decided we had better go back in and 'shape up.' Margaret was a wonderful friend."

Mother never got over her inability to stop laughing. Once she got started, she would giggle so hard that her face would turn red, and her body would shake all over. Watching her laugh was often funnier than the thing we were all laughing about. We would be pulled into her laugh-a-thon, and then we would all have tears streaming down our cheeks.

My mother had a wonderful, lighthearted outlook on life. No matter what would happen to us, she would say, "You might as well laugh at it now, because you know you are going to laugh at it later!" Her formula was: Tragedy + Time = Comedy. And she found a lot of comedy in life!

TOM, OLIVE, TOMMY & VERA DAVIS

OLIVE OSMOND

OLIVE DAVIS – AGE SIXTEEN

CHAPTER FIVE

UNDERSTANDING

Nineteen thirty-nine started like any other school year. My mother said that she was so glad to be in high school, where she could be part of a band and play her saxophone. She loved her sax and all of her closest associates whom she met in that band class. Everything seemed normal. They had just moved to Thatcher for the school months from Mount Pleasant. Then the world changed.

At first she did not understand what was happening. She walked down the school hallway and saw a teacher pass by her crying. In the school office, everyone was talking in hushed tones. When she got home, she found her father sitting beside their Philco radio listening very carefully to the scratchy voice of a reporter talking about something that had happened in a place called Poland. He mentioned the word "invasion" and something about a man called "Hitler," and then there was the word, "war."

UNDERSTANDING

It all seemed surreal and so far away from their cozy existence in Idaho. It was so difficult for Olive to comprehend how this was going to affect her or her family. The invasion of Poland was on the other side of the ocean. They were safe here in the mountains. But as time went on and everyone sat and listened to the radio, she could not dismiss the descriptions of war that came flooding in. People could not talk about anything else.

Then the community began to debate if America should get involved in the overseas conflict. Old veterans shook their heads in dismay. World War I was supposed to have been the war that ended all wars. Germany was not supposed to threaten anyone again.

All the peace and security that my mother had ever known in her childhood started to unravel as Germany continued its aggression. When they attacked England, it became clear that Germany and Hitler were intent upon expansion and domination. At school, some of the young male students talked with much bravado about how they hoped the war would last until they got out of school, so they could go and fight. Many of those same boys never waited for graduation. Their fate was sealed when Japan entered the fray and struck Pearl Harbor on December 7, 1941. Immediately after that, on December 8, the United States declared war on Japan and on Germany on December 11.

Mother's brother, Tommy, was too young to really know what was going on, so Tom and Vera thought it best not to talk about it around him. He was only five. Mother,, on the other hand, was old enough to have many questions: Why are Germany and Japan doing this? They bombed Hawaii—will they bomb the United States? Will they bomb Idaho? Will you, Father, have to go to war? My cousins? My uncles?

Then news began to leak out of Europe about concentration camps and about the round-up of Jewish people simply because of their religious beliefs. Nothing was known yet about what happened in the camps, with the eventual extermination of six million Jews. But each day reports on the radio were doleful.

My mother struggled to be hopeful about her future. She tried to study and attend school like she had, but that was impossible. No one could talk about anything except the war. She and her friends found moments of relief when they headed to a weekend movie where, for that moment, they could escape into another world. They went to dances and other school activities to try to keep a sense of normalcy, but the war overshadowed everything.

It came to Thatcher when military personnel brought notices of the soldiers' deaths arrived at the various homes in the community. And then they had to cope with the grieving families and funerals with flag-draped coffins.

There were nights when Mother lay in her bed alone and prayed and wept for all the suffering that was going on. She was afraid. She was having a hard time finding comfort or hope. Finally she came to her father—her one source of strength and clarity. On a quiet fall evening after Tommy had gone to bed, Olive could hold in her emotions no longer, so she turned to him and said, "Why do people hate? Why do they want to hurt each other? Why can't they live in peace? Why does God let this happen?"

My grandfather put his arms around her, and she wept on his shoulder. Her body shook with her broken sobs. He knew to just hold her and let her release all the anguish that she had stored. Then he gave her his handkerchief, lifted her chin so that she was looking into his eyes and said, "God cannot control a man's choices. It is not his plan to force his children to choose what is right. He gives us free agency and correct principles, and he allows us to choose for ourselves. We are often affected by the consequences of another person's wrong choice. And when that person is in a position to affect many by his or her choices, then many can be hurt."

"Then why doesn't God stop them?" she begged.

"He can't," Tom replied. "Each person in this life must choose for himself the path that he will follow. You cannot control what another person does to you. But you can control how you will react to it. You can be angry, bitter and vengeful, or you can forgive and depend on the Lord that He will, in his own time and in his own way, intervene."

"But so many people are suffering, and so many are dying! It just hurts so much!" was her retort.

Her father said, in his soothing voice, "Men have suffered and died in wars before over the centuries for many reasons. It is the nature of mortal life that there will always be opposition and those that want to control the lives of others. We came to this life to be tested by our Father in Heaven to see if we would remain obedient and true and faithful to our covenants, no matter what tests and trials we experience."

Quoting Mormon scripture, her father then said, "Ye cannot behold with your natural eyes, for the present time, the design of your God concerning those things which shall come hereafter, and the glory which shall follow after much tribulation. For, after much tribulation come the blessings."

My mother was faced with a choice at that moment. She could sink into the despair that was called forth in that time of national and international madness or find the strength to believe that her future and the future of the world's citizens could contain happiness and peace—that the present suffering was only temporary. But for now, she had to find peace in her heart—the peace that comes from trusting in the Lord.

To underscore her decision, her father added, "Remember, Olive, what the Lord said: 'Peace I leave with you, my peace I give unto you: not as the world giveth give I unto you. Let not your heart be troubled, neither let it be afraid.'"

And that was the day that my mother made her decision and found her strength. No longer was she a giddy teenager. She responded to the call to stand up and be spiritually counted.

The war continued to rage. Men died. Families grieved. Countries suffered. Whole ethnic populations were eliminated. Beginning with that day, my mother chose to cope with it all and to move forward with faith. This is same faith that she taught us and nurtured within us, and this is the same faith that sustained her to the end of her life.

OLIVE OSMOND

GEORGE

GEORGE OSMOND, circa 1944

CHAPTER SIX

GEORGE

By the time my mother was nineteen, she was working at the Adjutant General Depot in the old Scowcroft Building in Ogden, Utah which had been converted into offices. The war was still raging, and the military services were using about any building they could find. During World War II, Ogden became a significant hub and center for government agencies and war industries. An aggressive Ogden Chamber of Commerce had even convinced the government to build Hill Air Force Base in the Ogden area in 1938. During the war years, Ogden was considered a safe interior area with an excellent system of rail connections to move needed war materials to the war zones. As a result, the Naval Supply Depot was built in Clearfield and the Utah General Depot in Ogden. Even the United States Forest Service Regional Office was located in Ogden. And there were German and Italian prisoners of war interned in camps in the area. In its heyday during World War II, as many as 119 passenger trains passed through Ogden every twenty-four hours. This is the active military and government environment that Mother lived in when her family came to Utah.

Like a lot of young women, she had volunteered to assist the war effort after graduating from high school. She became a secretary and worked with about ten other girls in the office of a Mr. Wagner. One of their duties was to cut typewritten stencils on which were written addresses of different posts to which they would ship training manuals out to the troops.

On January 10, 1944, one of her co-workers, Belva Fluckiger, came walking into the office with a handsome young man in a tan army uniform. She introduced him to everyone as George Virl Osmond from Star Valley, Wyoming. Belva had once been his teacher in school. She then announced to the increasingly interested secretarial pool that he had just been released from the Army and was going to be working here at the depot. And of course, she made a point of telling them that George was single.

Mother recalled "The only way that I can explain my reaction to meeting him was 'love at first sight. I only saw him for a moment, but there was that smile and that mischievous glint in his eyes."

That evening my mother was working overtime, doing some bookkeeping for the Post Restaurant when George, who was eight years her senior, opened the door and peeked in. As he strode across the room, he sang out, "Hi, Jo. Are you working hard?"

She responded, "Nope, I'm hardly working." (That was the first time that she had ever been called "Jo," a slang nominative of the day, but she liked it coming from him.)

George noticed the grey- and black-striped pen she was using and said, "Well, look at that! We have pens just alike. I'll bet my pen has traveled farther than your pen!"

Mother laughed and said, "I'm sure it has because my pen hasn't traveled very far at all. I was born in Idaho. So far I've been to Washington and Oregon, and now I'm in Utah. I haven't seen California yet."

He laughed and told her he had been born in Star Valley, Wyoming but spent quite a bit of his youth in San Diego, California and just got back from serving overseas where he had been stationed in England.

As Mother looked back on this initial moment with George, she said it was not like any other encounter she had ever had. Being in the presence of this particular man made her dizzy and warm all over.

That night, my mother remembered that her mother, Vera, and her Aunt Dora had lived and taught school in Star Valley before they were married, so she asked, "Mom, did you ever know any Osmonds from Star Valley?"

"Why, yes," she replied. "I lived with some Osmonds. Dora and I stayed with a young widow named LaVerna Osmond. She had three little boys. Their father was killed when he was kicked by a horse, and she took us in as boarders to help provide for them. I think I might even have a picture of them."

She went to her closet and found two old photos. One was of George and the other was of him with his brothers. Olive stared in disbelief. She was amazed her mother had these, and she was excited to show them to George the next time she saw him.

The next day Mother took the pictures to work with her. She saw George waiting in the lunch line at the Post Restaurant. She walked up to him and asked, "Would you like to see something interesting?" as she handed him the pictures.

George looked at them and got a puzzled expression on his face. Then he turned them over and saw "George Virl Osmond" written on the back. His jaw dropped and he gasped, "Why, that's my mother's handwriting! Where did you get these?"

Mother explained about her mother and Aunt Dora living in Star Valley as teachers and boarding at his mother's home. His eyebrows rose. He looked at Olive a moment, recovered his composure and said, "My mother would be delighted to see these because her pictures were all destroyed in a fire."

One of the employees at the Post Restaurant said that he had a photo lab in Logan, Utah. So, Mother decided to give him the two precious photos and have him make some copies for her and George. In an ironic and sad twist, he lost them and they never saw the pictures again.

One of my mother's duties was to take care of the cash register at the restaurant during lunch time. Sometimes, when they were especially busy, she would also dip ice cream cones as well. She was working there one day when my father came through the line. She casually slipped him an extra scoop of ice cream. He smiled and winked. Later she learned that ice cream was one of his passions.

A few days later they ran into each other. They were making small talk when George suddenly asked, "Do you like to dance?"

"I love to dance," she replied a little too enthusiastically.

"Would you go with me to the White City Ballroom Saturday night? There's a big band coming to town. My friend, Tim Jessop, and his wife Phyllis are going, too. How would it be if we picked you up about 6:00 PM to have some dinner and go dancing?'

"That would be wonderful!" Mother replied. She tried to return to her work, but she said that she was so excited, she was trembling.

George picked her up in a blue Oldsmobile he had just bought. He was so pleased with that car. It was used, but he had worked on it until it was shining like a mirror. They were supposed to meet the other couple at Kay's Noodle Parlor, but they arrived a bit early so George suggested that they stop for a soda first.

Mother always told the part about getting out of the car and walking in next to him as being wildly romantic. A fall breeze was blowing softly. She had a white, lacy scarf around her head. As they walked in, they heard a song playing on the jukebox called "Who." It was the first song they had ever heard together. She listened to the lyrics and thought, "How romantic they are." Later she tried desperately to find the music so she could have the lyrics, but she never was able to locate it.

The Jessops finally joined them, and George introduced her to *chow mein*, a first for a small-town girl. There was still time for a movie before the dance, so the four went to see "Abbott and Costello in Society." They laughed a lot and were introduced to another song they both could not get out of their heads. They hummed it and sang parts of it all the rest of the evening. It was called, "My Dreams Are Getting Better All the Time." The key lyrics go like this:

To think that we were strangers
A couple of nights ago
An' though it's a dream, I never dreamed
He'd ever say hello.
Oh, maybe tonight
I'll hold him tight
When the moonbeams shine
My dreams are getting better all the time.

As I said, my mother danced a lot during high school, but she had never danced with the likes of George Osmond. Then and there, she decided he was the best dancer she had ever had the privilege of being with. He was so light on his feet and had such great rhythm. He had a little trick step that tripped her up a few times, but she finally mastered it. They danced all evening (except when the band performed solo pieces, when they stood on the sidelines and just watched). She did not remember which big band was playing but she was sure that it was Margaret Whiting who was the featured singer.

Part of the ballroom was actually outside, so they danced there also and looked up at the bountiful star-filled heavens, all the while being serenaded by the romantic sounds of a waterfall. There could not have been a more perfect moment. They held each other and sensed that something special was happening between the both of them.

George had spent three years in the Army in England. He enlisted in August of 1941, even before the Pearl Harbor attack. On his enlistment papers it said that he was a carpenter with a year of college. Before that, he had been in the CCC which was a public works program set up to provide relief for the unemployed resulting from the Great Depression. This was done by implementing a general natural resource conversation program on lands across the country. It became one of the popular New Deal programs sponsored by Franklin Roosevelt which provided economic relief, rehabilitation and training for three million men.

Typical work projects included: structural improvement like bridges and fire towers; transportation improvement to truck routes, foot trails and air landing fields; erosion and food control; planting trees and shrubs; and fire prevention and fire fighting.

Normally, a nineteen-year-old young Mormon male would prepare for and go on a mission for the church for a two- or three-year period. But, World War II disrupted that program for all the young LDS men, so George became a typical CCC enrollee—an unmarried, unemployed male, 18-25 years of age. Each enrollee volunteered and, upon passing a physical exam, was signed up for a six-month term with the option to serve as much as two years. He lived in the work camp and received $30 a month as well as food, clothing and medical care.

Even though my father had gone from the CCC to army service in World War II and was now working at the Depot in Ogden, he was not ready to settle down. He had no money, and he wanted to get his feet on the ground first. He wanted to have a bank account and some real job security. He became disillusioned with the money he was making at the Adjutant General Depot when he found out what he could make as a brakeman on the Southern Pacific Railroad.

My mother and father did not see each other very often after that. She complained in her journal, "It seemed he was always working. His work at the railroad was irregular. Sometimes he would be gone more than a day, and then he would have a day at home. But on those days home he would drive a taxi, so he was working most of the time!" Mother's parents were actually relieved that the romance had cooled down. They thought she was too young to get married.

One night, after George had driven an officer to Brigham City, he stopped by to see Mother on his way home. She had just made an angel food cake and he gladly helped himself to several slices of it. It was the first time that he had met her mother and father and little brother, Tommy. George immediately brought up the Star Valley boarding incident and Vera shared that the two women had become good friends while she was there. They laughed at the amazing coincidence, and George promised to try and bring his mother to Ogden, so they could renew their acquaintance.

He then noticed a line-up of sheet music on the piano and asked Olive if she would play him one of the songs. He stood behind her as she played, putting his hand on her shoulders and started to sing the lyrics. My mother said, "Chills went up and down my spine as I listened to his voice. It was so beautiful and mellow. It caught the attention of my family, too, and they told me later how they moved their chairs close to the kitchen door so they could hear him. Wow, I thought, this guy is handsome; he can dance and sing too? He's melting my heart right away."

Mother tried to find out as much as she could about my father, but he was not very open about his life. All she could figure out was that it had been hard. She struggled to understand how someone who seemed so talented and suave could be hiding something so difficult that he did not want to talk about it.

In spite of her crush on him, my mother could not get George to come around more often than he did. Belva kept her up-to-date about his comings and goings, since he was boarding at her home. Occasionally he would stop by my mother's house and sing a song or two. Sometimes she would not be there when he came by, and she would be crestfallen that she had missed him. As time passed, George would ask her on an occasional date. Then one night, Mother got to hear what she was longing for. They had just been to a movie, and they were sitting in the car in front of her house. George said, "Olive, you are just the kind of woman that I've been looking for. I think that I want to marry you, but I don't have enough money in the bank or a good enough job to take on that responsibility just yet."

That moment was not as romantic as she had hoped, but it would do. She was completely smitten. As an idealistic nineteen-year-old, she protested, "I don't care if you do not have enough money, we can get by."

But George was adamant. He had been on his own, scraping by since he was fifteen, and he was determined that his marriage was not going to be launched into that kind of poverty. So, she backed off, content that he had at least asked her to marry him, and tried to wait patiently.

Then things began to unravel. While George was working at the rail yard, he stepped off a train while it was still moving, (it was something that he had done many times before) but this time, he caught his foot on something and fell. The train was going so fast, it threw him off and down an embankment. He injured his foot quite severely.

Belva carried the news of his injury to Mother at work, and she immediately left for Belva's house. When she walked in, George was sitting with his foot in a tub of hot water. He was quite surprised and a little embarrassed to have her see him in that condition. But Mother fussed over him, while he nervously tried to hide that he had been tooling a rhinestone pattern onto a leather motorcycle belt, while tending to his injury. He was not ready to tell her that he had sold his car and bought a Harley motorcycle.

George's foot finally healed, and he called to ask if she wanted to go out for a chicken dinner at his friends' place up Ogden Canyon. She was delighted with the idea, but when he roared up on a big Harley Davidson, which had a "buddy seat," thirteen lights and lots of gadgets, she was stunned.

He hopped off and proudly strutted around it, pointing out its great features. Finally Mother asked where his car was. He admitted he had traded it in for the motorcycle. She was crestfallen. *How could we ever date now?* She wondered.

She certainly had no intention of riding on the back of that thing! But my father was a very persuasive man and sweet-talked her into riding behind him, promising he would be very careful. Reluctantly, she got on.

He said, "Hold tight!" and with a screech of the wheels they were off. He hit some loose gravel on the way up the canyon and nearly dumped them. Though Mother felt she was well out of her comfort zone, when the ride was over, she had to admit that she had a really good time.

But motorcycles were not meant for courting grounded girls like my mother. It was only a matter of time before something went wrong. George and his friend Chick decided to ride their motorcycles to Star Valley, Wyoming. Chick's wife, Vergie and Olive followed them up in their car. The women got there long before the men did, but it was only a matter of time before they began to worry about them. It started to get quite late when George finally pulled up alone. He said that Chick had been in an accident and was in the hospital. Vergie panicked and raced out the door to the hospital to be with him. He apparently had something blow into his face, blocking his nose and mouth, and causing him to black out. His motorcycle went out of control, veered off the road and over an embankment.

While there in Star Valley, my mother finally got to meet George's mother, LaVerna and his younger half-sister, Cora. She now knew where George got his laughing eyes and energetic personality. LaVerna Osmond was a strong-willed and determined lady who had survived the loss of three husbands and still had a positive, happy view of life. She shared many stories with the intently interested young woman.

Finally, it grew late, and Cora and Mother went upstairs to sleep. They watched the stars twinkle through the gaps in the roof of the cabin. They continued to talk halfway through the night. My mother enjoyed learning more about George from her. Cora said she called him her "knight in shining armor" and told Mother how good he had always been to her. She did not need any more to convince her that he was a wonderful man, but that was a nice icing on the cake.

Chick stayed in the hospital overnight and then was released. He was actually well enough to drive home on his motorcycle. Vergie and Mother drove as far as Montpelier, Idaho with the boys following behind.

Then George asked her to ride with him on the motorcycle for awhile, which she did. He put his goggles on her and, with her hanging on tightly to her "knight," off they went.

The trip gave Mother quite a sunburn. When she showed up at work the next day, she looked like a raccoon. Her face was bright red but her eyes were clown white where the goggles had been. Everyone, including her boss, had a good laugh.

And that was the end of the courtship for awhile. A few days later, George showed up at her house to say he was going to California to think things over and see if he could get a better job. He told Mother she was the kind of girl he had always hoped to find, but he reiterated the time was not right.

George then let his guard down, and she was shown the jagged interior of this outwardly handsome man. He finally shared with her some of the details of his unhappy childhood: the death of his father when he was just six weeks old; the remarriage of his mother to a less-than-favorable second husband; their move to California, then to Wyoming and a third stepfather who kicked him out, and how he had been on his own by the time he was fifteen.

He waited and watched her face. Nothing he had said had changed her adoring expression. So he took a deep breath and continued, "Look Olive, I'm afraid to getting married. I also have some health problems." Still there was no change, no shock or concern in her face. So he plunged on, "And you need to know that I had a nervous breakdown after the war. I saw things in England. It affected me. I didn't handle it too well. I don't ever want to be a burden to anyone."

Mother placed her hand on his and said, "Do you believe that God brought us together?" My father was taken off guard by the question.

"George," she said, "from the moment we met, you were different from anyone that I have ever known. I kept asking the Lord why we came together and why I liked you so much. When I would try to dismiss you from my mind, you would come back in my thoughts even stronger. I don't know what the future holds or what tests and trials we will face. But I do know this: I am supposed to be your wife. Now you need to get your own confirmation. Once you have it, nothing else in the world will matter."

George stared long and silent into her eyes. Then he gathered his things, gave her a quick kiss on the cheek and left. He did not say anything about coming back. Staring at the closed door, Mother sat down and sobbed. She was devastated. She thought maybe he really didn't love her after all. She had never known anyone like George Osmond and now she thought that she had lost him.

GEORGE – 26 YEARS OLD

MR. AND MRS. GEORGE VIRL OSMOND

CHAPTER SEVEN

ETERNAL MARRIAGE

To understand my parent's relationship, it is important to understand my father's early years and what incidents made him struggle emotionally. My mother served as his anchor and support throughout those first years of their married life. Because she lived a rather idyllic childhood, she had a strong sense of commitment to life and work. She was actively engaged in what was going on around her and believed in her ability to influence events in her life. She enjoyed new challenges and was not afraid of the future.

In contrast, when I look at my father's early life, it saddens me to see what he had to endure. At first he was so reluctant to make a commitment to my mother. He had a history of moving from place to place, never allowing himself to get attached to people. Events and experiences of his past haunted him. My father suffered from what is today known as PTSD (post-traumatic stress disorder.) For him, it was caused in part by a difficult childhood and being a first-hand witness and participant in the horrors of war.

After his father was killed in a horse accident when he was six weeks old, his mother, LaVerna, moved her little family around about ten different times until he finally felt he was old enough and he left home. They had moved from Star Valley, Wyoming to Burley, Idaho and then to Ogden, Utah. From there they lived in Los Angeles and San Diego and then back to Wyoming. This was in an era when a young widow was very limited in finding a means of supporting herself and family.

My father wrote in his journal: "In San Diego, we lived on the edge of a canyon where there were a lot of loquat trees. We had a dog named Mickey that our neighbor did not like very well. One day he fed him some food with ground glass in it, and we all watched him die."

In another entry he said his brother Rulon and Ralph had a paper route. "I always helped them. At three o'clock every morning we were folding papers on a street corner. One morning we looked up and I watched a big plane in the sky crash into a smaller plane. The big plane spun around in a circle and then plunged into the canyon."

George's mother eventually remarried. His new step-father had part ownership in a bakery in Los

Angeles. He was not a very demonstrative man and didn't show his feelings that much. He compensated for this awkwardness by being a person who teased and played practical jokes on people.

Father remembered riding down with him to Tijuana, Mexico. His step-father traveled there often and was well-acquainted with the guards at the border. He thought it would be funny to tell them that George had been drinking. So the guards made him walk a chalk line. It was all in fun, but my father was terrified and humiliated.

He seemed to be the butt of everyone's jokes. One time his Uncle John and Aunt Ruth and their family were staying with them, and his cousin Helen locked him in his pigeon coop where he remained stuck for the rest of the day.

In another example from his journal: "We used to take the young squab and have a cookout in the back yard and fry the chicken eggs. Ralph had a BB gun and told Rulon that he was going to shoot the next chicken that came around the corner of the coop. Well, it happened to be my pet chicken and did I cry!"

His first stepfather unsuccessfully gambled on a number of money-making enterprises, including gold mining. My father said, "When the vein ran out, he seemed to suffer a breakdown and lose touch with reality. He started stepping out on Mother. When she found out about it, she left him and we moved back to Wyoming. Mother took a little house in Thayne and tried to hold her family together. My stepfather followed her and tried to mend his fences, but she would have nothing to do with him."

Soon his mother took a job as a housekeeper for a widower who lived in Fairview, Wyoming. He had five children. So his mother became a very busy woman. Besides the housework, she also milked the cows for him. Father's older brothers were sent to live with relatives, so she was there alone with George and her five new charges.

After a couple of years the two left this man's employ and moved down into Burley, Idaho. But he followed her and talked her into marriage even though my father protested vigorously. LaVerna eventually married him. George and his second step-father never got along. Finally by the time he was fifteen, he left home and was supporting himself with odd jobs.

In spite of living on his own, my father managed to graduate from Star Valley High School in 1936. Just before graduation, a friend talked him into joining the Civilian Conservation Corp or CCC. He took the examination and was inducted, but his friend failed the exam, so he had to go in alone. By then, he and his second stepfather were not even on speaking terms.

The CCC became a respite from this nomadic and difficult life. Both his older brothers had served a hitch in the CCC ahead of him, and he went into the same camp that his brother Ralph had just left. Ralph was a cook and also represented the camp in boxing. He had made a good name for himself, so my father was well accepted on Ralph's laurels.

Rather than dig ditches or fight fires, he wound up being assigned charge of the recreation room and spent his time racking pool balls and cleaning up the place. In his spare time he bought a little recording machine and learned to play the guitar and sing a few songs. Later he was reassigned to the job of "Dog Robber." This meant he served the commissioned officers their meals. It was also his job to take care of his division's office, so in his spare time he learned to type and even do a little shorthand.

Father had injured his back some years before in an accident and while in the CCC he found out that he needed surgery to correct some damage it caused to his spine. My father was sent to the Cheyenne Army Post where he not only had this operation, but had his tonsils out at the same time! His recovery was rough and he endured it alone.

Then came America's involvement in World War II and his subsequent assignment stationed in London, England. While there, he witnessed many bombings and destruction as he worked in the shipyards at the supply depot. When his war years were over, he was mustered out of the service and went home suffering from posttraumatic stress disorder.

Besides the multitude of traumatic events he experienced in England during the war that lead to his PTSD, my father was struggling with self-esteem and abandonment issues and was not coping with them very well at the time. In my father's journals were many entries that seemed like pleadings with the Lord for relief from the shadows and memories that haunted him. They were heartfelt and painful.

For years he had bad dreams. He felt fearful and nervous. It was difficult for him to stop thinking about events of the past. His condition is recognized in the military today among soldiers who have experienced the horrors of war, but in 1944 there were no medications or access to therapy. Most men just hid their interior terrors, then tried to work hard and move on with life. My father was no different. But then he had the great good fortune to meet and fall in love with Olive Davis.

Mother tried to cope with the loneliness of my father's absence by working long hours with lots of overtime. She even took a correspondence course in dress design and went to night school at a business college for awhile. She frequently played the saxophone in a dance band on the base. She dated a few other young men but was happier just concentrating on her work. She trained new secretaries, and her boss gave her a raise whenever he was allowed to by government regulations. She wrote: "I kept very busy but I missed him so."

Finally, a letter came from George with a little "slave chain" inside. It was a popular trinket at the time worn around the ankle. The letter said he was lying on the beach thinking about his life and wondering if she would like to share the rest of it with him.

She said that she clutched the chain to her heart and then put it on immediately. She was so happy to finally hear from him again, but she wondered if he was serious. Words are cheap when they come from eight hundred miles away in San Diego. She had been hurt and teased by co-workers about being "jilted" by George taking off the way that he did. She vacillated about accepting his offer and then decided she would keep her "slave chain" gift private along with any other correspondence she got from him, just to be safe.

Then several weeks later, Belva called in the evening and asked my mother if she would go on a blind date with one of her friends who was coming into town. She said she was tired and really did not want to go. Belva begged and pleaded. She said she owed this guy a favor. She said he was kind of a special guy, and she was sure that she would enjoy the evening. Belva came over to help "doll up" a new black dress that mother had just bought by sewing sequins around the trim and down the front. She liked the end result but wondered why Belva was being so helpful.

Later Belva called and said she was sending someone over to pick her up. By the time her "chauffeur" arrived, she was thinking about calling the date off. She decided she just was not up to it. Then she heard a knock at the back door. Thinking it was a someone for her father, she plodded through the kitchen and answered it. It was George!

"I was in a state of shock!" she wrote in her journal. "But I was also a little angry. Why hadn't Belva told me she was sending him to pick me up? So I told him sarcastically that I had a date."

He said, 'Belva sent me over to get you. By the way, what's my best girl doing dating some other guy?'"

She gave him a dark look and walked out the door. Over her shoulder, she shot out angrily, "I didn't think you cared!"

On the short drive over to Belva's, she stewed. *How could Belva be so insensitive as to ask George to bring me over to her house? Does my blind date not even have a car?*

Father, on the other hand, had a slight smirk on his face all the way to Belva's place. He walked around and opened the car door for her, then escorted her to the front door. She thought, *How awkward this is going to be!*

Then he turned the door knob and pushed it open. Mother saw that they were the only ones there. Soft music was playing on the radio, and a candlelit table for two was set in the living room. She could also see dinner already prepared on the stove in the kitchen.

Then Father admitted, "Olive, I'm the date Belva set you up with. I did this, because I didn't know if you'd see me."

My mother was shocked. She had never written him back after he had sent her the chain. "We had a lovely dinner, "she said, "and visited for quite awhile. Then he asked me if I'd like to dance." She melted into his arms.

As he held her and danced across the room, he glided them over to the fireplace and said in a tender voice, "There's a present for you in back of that picture."

Mother remembered, "I opened the package and there was a beautiful diamond engagement ring inside! Then he asked me to marry him! After catching my breath, I said, YES!"

This was the romantic moment that she had dreamed about. Then George invited her to kneel down with him in Belva's front room and they said a prayer, hand in hand, and asked the Lord to guide and direct them as they moved forward with their lives together. At that moment, somewhere in heaven, nine spirits destined to come to earth as their children, shouted for joy. And the beginning of events that would bring the name Osmond world recognition was set in motion.

When Mother went home and told her parents the good news, she was surprised to find they did not seem too thrilled. They told her they thought she was too young to get married. They liked George, but they were worried about his commitment. However, they later decided to fast and pray about it and said they received an answer of peace and assurance.

She could not sleep all night. She kept the lamp on by her bedside and held out her ring finger under the light, fascinated by the different colors reflected in the little diamond. Now she felt free to share her relationship to George with the world. When she showed up at work the next day, wearing her treasure, it really caused some excitement. She was on cloud nine.

My parents prayed and felt that they should get married as soon as possible. They decided to get married in October, one month from their engagement, but Vera became quite ill, so they postponed it. Her mother's health improved in a few weeks, so they chose the first of December as the date they would aim for and started making preparations.

Eternal marriage is considered one of the highest covenants that Mormons can make with the Lord in their sacred temples. When a man and woman are married in the temple, they kneel across from each other at the altar, hold each other's hands, and their union is "sealed" for time and all eternity.

In order to be married in the temple, a couple must be clean and pure both temporally and spiritually, and worthy to enter into the House of the Lord. They first must have an interview with their ecclesiastical authority and verify their worthiness before they can receive a temple recommend which allows them to enter into the sacred edifice. Moral and religious standards are very strict in the church, and obedience to the Lord's commandments are taken very seriously.

Members of the Church of Jesus Christ of Latter-day Saints understand there will be challenges to overcome in their relationship. Eternal marriages do not just happen because one is married in the temple. Rather, an eternal marriage is a constant work in progress. My parents were nervous about the step that they were about to embark upon. They did not take it lightly, but they were filled with hope.

Mother looked all over Ogden and Salt Lake for that special wedding dress. Although she found a couple she liked, they were very expensive and definitely out of her budget range. Belva came to her rescue, again, and offered to make one for her if she would purchase the material. So, with Olive supervising, Belva made a wedding dress that was modest, simple and elegant.

She wrote, "I bought a pretty purple suit, a fuchsia coat, a black pill box hat with fuchsia feathers, black shoes and purse for my 'going away outfit' as it was referred to in those days. Those colors, purple and fuchsia, were very popular at that time, and I loved that outfit." (They remained one of her favorite color combinations throughout her life.)

She also had a hope chest. It was made of cedar and a popular tradition for young women of the day. It contained items which she had been collecting since she was a young girl. There were some heirloom dishes, family pictures, a Bible with pages to record births, marriages, and deaths. And there were two sets of embroidered pillow cases. She wanted to have more in it by then, but the war was on and made even practical items like sheets hard to come by.

As the time grew nearer for the wedding date, Olive's mother fell ill again and had to go to the hospital for gall bladder surgery. She was adamant that Olive and George go ahead with their temple marriage, even though she could not be there. My mother was so torn. She did not know what to do, so she went to her father for advice. He encouraged her to go ahead with their plans for marriage. He, however, would have to remain at the hospital by his wife's bedside. But they promised her that their hearts and prayers would be with them. Later Mother said, "Well, it wasn't much of a wedding, but we made it a wonderful marriage."

The night before their wedding, the two went to the hospital and took Vera a flower. They had a long talk. "She was so sweet and was glad to see us so happy together," Mother said. "She reassured us we were doing the right thing. I worried about both my parents and my little brother, Tom. Would they be lonesome without me? After all, I had lived at home with them all of my life and now I was leaving them."

George's mother, LaVerna, came down from Star Valley, Wyoming and stayed with Olive that night. The soon-to-be bride could not sleep at all and found herself suddenly filled with doubt and confusion. She was marrying a man so very different from herself; her parents could not be there with them in the temple— what was she doing? She burst into tears, and she knelt by her bed and prayed to the Lord to comfort her mind. She had fasted and prayed about marrying George once before and had received a confirmation he was the "one." Why was she so distraught now? Something inside of her said that this marriage was not going to be easy, that there would be many difficult challenges, and she was going to carry a heavy responsibility.

"Father, please," she pleaded, "I know I can meet any trial as both a wife and a mother if you are with me. Please just tell me this is right."

At that moment, she said that she felt a physical calm and peace come over her, and she heard in her mind one of her favorite scriptures: "Trust in the Lord with all thine heart; lean not unto thine own understanding. In all thy ways acknowledge Him, and He shall direct thy paths." (Proverbs 3:5,6)

The morning of December 1, 1944 finally came. My parents were married for time and all eternity in a beautiful sealing room of the Salt Lake City, Utah temple. The chandelier-dominated room had two large mirrors on either side that reflected the image of the couple across the altar, over and over into infinity—

representing the eternal nature of their marriage covenant. They knelt across at the altar, clasped hands and together, in front of the marriage officiator, Robert I. Burton, Belva's uncle, made everlasting promises to each other and before the witnesses who were in attendance. After the ceremony, they celebrated by going to their favorite Noodle Parlor where they dined on Chinese noodles.

Their wedding reception was scheduled for a week later in Ogden, in hopes that her mother would be well enough to stand in the receiving line. Once again Belva, came to the couple's rescue. It was she who made arrangements for refreshments, flowers, and a lovely cake that sat on a mirror over in the corner of the room. She even had her brother there, taking photos for them.

Vera could hardly stand up, but she put on a brave face and, with interval rests, was able to stand most of the time in the reception line. Mother later wrote in her journal, "I could not believe so many people came to our reception. Dad and Mother had invited their relatives and friends, George's folks had invited theirs, and George and I had invited ours. We really had a lot of people go through the line that night."

Their honeymoon was cut short, because they both had to get back to work. They moved into a little cinder block apartment at U-13 Bonneville Park in Ogden, Utah.

Like everything else in my mother's life up to this time, her circumstances were humble and simple. Right away the couple decided they needed to have a special focus to guide them spiritually, so they chose a scripture they liked (D&C 88:119) and made a copy of it and hung it on the wall. It read:

"Organize yourselves; prepare every needful thing;
and establish a house, even a house of prayer,
a house of fasting, a house of faith, a house of learning,
a house of glory,
a house of order, a house of God."

That scripture proved to be a spiritual anchor for both of them. My father made it his duty to keep our home organized in all respects of the word. His commitment to organization and order and Mother's to faith, prayer and learning influenced and strengthened our lives for decades to come.

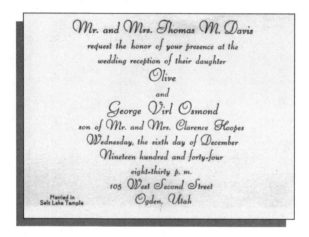

NEWLYWED OSMONDS IN OGDEN

CHAPTER EIGHT
NESTING

My parents rented their little apartment at U-13 Bonneville Park shortly before they were married, so it was ready to move into when they came home from Salt Lake. These were tiny cinder block buildings built during the war to take care of the overflow of military personnel. Father qualified because he had been in the military, and my mother because she worked for the Adjutant General's Office.

They moved her bed, dresser and the cedar chest into the apartment. "George's folks gave us a nice kitchen set—a table and four chairs—for a wedding present, so we had a full house." There was a small, black, coal-burning pot-belly stove to heat the apartment. The house also came with a small ice box— literally—no refrigerator. "What a chore that was to keep ice in it and empty the pan below when it melted. Sometimes we would forget to empty the pan before we left for work and had to mop the floor when we got home."

NESTING

The bathroom was tiny—no tub—just a shower. "We added curtains to the bedroom and a lovely round white rug. We put this by our bed and always knelt on it to say our prayers. I had a lace-trimmed beige dresser scarf on the dresser, and one morning I noticed George had written on it with a pencil, 'I love you, honey!' I embroidered it with red thread as a keepsake."

For their first Christmas they bought a little tree and made the decorations themselves. Because of the war, there were no electric lights available, so they trimmed the tree with cellophane strips by twisting them in the middle to make bows. They then crushed some old broken ornaments to make their own "glitter" and glued the glitter to each end of the bows. "The tree was cute, and we had fun being creative."

While the war was being fought, the government rationed a number of items, including gas, shoes and sugar. Other items were in short supply, like bed sheets and irons. In fact, the couple did not have an iron. One morning they heard on the radio that the local store just received a shipment of steam irons. Sales were based on a first-come, first-served basis. They dashed downtown and bought one. The problem was that Mother was in the early stages of pregnancy, and every time she used it, she became nauseous. "It had a peculiar smell that literally made me ill, so I had to put it away until after the baby was born."

After a few months, they purchased two acres on Wall Avenue, a few houses away from Mother's parents. They planned to build a home there, where they could have a garden, fruit trees, berries, chickens, and other elements of a farm that she missed. They could not wait for spring to come. When it did, "we went out with a tape measure and we measured every inch of it."

An important provision of the G.I. Bill was low interest, zero down payment home loans for servicemen. This enabled millions of American families like my parents to move out of urban apartments and into suburban homes.

Armed with a house plan that Mother had picked out in high school as her "dream home," they decided to build a "basement house" and build on top later when they could afford it. Because my father wanted to spend as much time as possible working on it after his day job, and because my mother did not have much to do since she quit work—she was ill most of the time with pregnancy—her parents invited the couple to take a room in their home (105 West Second Street) and stay there until they could move into their basement house.

"They were so good to us. They always liked to hear George sing. He had a lovely voice, so in the evenings I would usually play a few songs and he would sing—just like we did when we were dating."

NESTING

Father was becoming more and more disillusioned with the job he had making wooden boxes at a box factory. He had sufficient savings in the bank, so he quit and concentrate on building the house.

"We could hardly wait to get started. I can still remember the excitement I felt when the big back hoe came in and dug the basement."

Since he had learned the building trade and had helped his older brother, Ralph, build many homes, he was confident that he knew just what had to be done. So he hired local men to help him set the forms, and the Osmond home was on its way. However, after the cement had all been poured, Father discovered he had made a bad mistake. He had forgotten to block out a place for the window in the bathroom.

"I was so disappointed, I actually cried," Mother wrote. "This was supposed to be my dream home and already it was ruined." But her sweetheart came up with a clever solution. He made a window in the bathroom wall right next to the bedroom, which was still pretty close to where it should have been.

"The basement was a cute little place. We had four rooms and a small bathroom with a shower (still no tub). George had built some pretty archways rather than doors between the living room and kitchen and between the living room and hall. That helped the heat to circulate better, and it also looked very nice. He had a plasterer come in and put a nice finish on the walls. We papered the living room with a beige embossed wallpaper. It had a gold flower in it that reflected light. Additionally, George tiled the floor throughout with brown and beige tiles. Finally we bought me a Double-Dexter washer ('my pride and joy')."

Mother was smitten with nesting. She bought a bassinet and placed it next to the heater in the corner where it would be "toasty warm" for the new baby.

The room at the foot of the stairs was reserved for a storage room. Father built shelves on the west side of it, and they began putting away cans of food and staples. (Latter-day Saints have been asked to put aside enough money and food to be able to survive minimally for at least three months. Self-sufficiency and provident living is a principle that has been taught in the Mormon Church for a long time. It helps to buffer a family's life when stresses occur, such as unemployment long-term illness, or a regional disaster, assisting the family to bridge the gap between lean and good economic times.

"I'll never forget George's comment the night we ate our first meal in our new house," my mother wrote. "This is something I've looked forward to all my life—being able to put my feet under my own table."

NESTING

When World War II came to an end in the Pacific arena, the troops came home, and the country was in an energetic and spirited mood. Babies were born at an all-time high rate (later to tagged as "baby boomers"). Between December, 1945 and December, 1947, cost of goods rose about one-third, as people drove up the prices, vying for scarce consumer goods. They had savings, because they were not able to spend all they made during the war due to rationing.

Economists had assumed that there would be a post-war depression, instead there was a post-war boom. The United States had grown even richer. The New Deal and wartime policies of high taxes and high wages had redistributed incomes, giving the average person the ability to buy.

It was in this climate that Father decided, after nearly finishing the "house" and running out of money, that it was time to look for another job. He was fighting PTSD—suffering bouts of anxiety and depression. It did not help that Olive was sick most of the time.

The two rallied and looked through the newspapers until Mother found an ad from the local radio station, KLO, looking for salesmen for their advertising department. She showed it to Father who immediately said, "No, I am no salesman."

She retorted, "How do you know that? Have you ever tried selling?"

He admitted he had not but did not like the idea. Mother persisted, "It wouldn't hurt to go and talk to them and see what it is all about, sweetheart."

He gave in. When he came home, he said, "That job is open, but I don't want it. I still don't think I'm cut out for that sort of thing. If that guy (the station manager) calls, just tell him I'm not home and that I'll probably be gone for two or three days. Maybe by then they'll find someone else."

"Well, 'that guy' called all right," Mother wrote. "His name was Frank Call, and he said, "Mrs. Osmond, we've found our man. That husband of yours is just the guy we've been looking for. He's as friendly as a pup, and we want him to start working as soon as possible."

She told him her husband was not home (which was true), but then she deviated from being the obedient wife—something she did later on occasions when she felt her intuition was right. She told him she would have him come in as soon as she saw him.

Father was not too happy about taking the job, but he had not found anything any better, so he thought he might as well give it a try. The station management suggested that he use the name "George" rather than his official first name, "Virl," because the business men could remember it better. So from then on, he was officially "George," and the name "Virl" would be reserved for me, their firstborn son.

Thus began the first of many highly successful working situations between my parents. Mother always loved office work and the training she had received at the business college and at the Depot. So she typed letters, did the accounting, set up a schedule for contacting the various clients and anything else she could do in her condition from their home-based office.

"We had a big piece of Celotex (about 4' x 6') which George hung on the wall, and we used it as a bulletin board. The radio station gave him a list of all the accounts he was supposed to service. I typed them alphabetically and posted it on the board. Then we got colored map tacks—six colors—one for each day of the week except Sunday, and we worked out a logical system which days he should contact the different businesses. When he left each morning, I would have a list all typed up for him." The radio station hired "George," but they also got Mother in the bargain.

Often Father had to help his clients write the copy that would be used on the air, so he would call Mother and together they would create the ads. Sometimes it was only a suggestion, but the business owners appreciated their help. "I remember a comment that was made to me by a man named Sam Herscovitz, the owner of Reliable Furniture Company, our largest account. He said, 'Do you know what I like about your husband? If he tells me he will be in Thursday afternoon with copy, I know he will be in Thursday afternoon!' That made me feel real good, because I knew my scheduling at home was helping him a little bit."

On the days my father had to drive for some distance, such as to Brigham City, Mother would go with him and read or work on copy for the radio advertising.

With this success, Mother got fired up about efficiency in general. One day she decided to "file" everything in the kitchen. She stacked dishes in the cupboards near the sink, so they could easily be put away. All her baking supplies (four, sugar, spices, flavorings, shortening) were put together in one end of the cabinet alphabetically; and underneath that area, she stacked the electric mixer, mixing bowls, baking pans in precise order. Even canned goods were sorted by vegetables, fruits, meats.

She really tried to be a good housekeeper, but her love for reading sometimes got in the way. In spite of the organizing, it was not beyond her to leave the dishes in the sink and sit down to read a good book. She was "literally digesting" a series of books called *Childcraft*.

With simple texts and illustrations, the volumes were designed to make learning fun. Each volume addressed different subjects, including literature—such as short stories and poetry, including fairy tales and nursery rhymes—as well as mathematics and the sciences. Now that she was going to be a mother, she wanted to learn all she could so she could teach her children.

Father got a little perturbed with her, though, when he came home to find the house in disarray. Mother admitted, "He loved to see the house nice and tidy at all times." But she felt cheated if she did not read every day. So sometimes soiled clothes were hidden in the closet, and dirty dishes were camouflaged under a towel on the sink, so she could steal time for learning and still keep my father happy.

One day they were invited to the home of Ford and Beulah Rose, who lived in South Ogden. Father and Ford worked together at KLO. The couple had seven children. My mother was fascinated listening to Beulah relate how she managed that many children. "She had some clever ideas." So, even though she was sick throughout this first pregnancy, she was already looking ahead to having her other eight babies.

They bought an old Chevrolet. By all accounts, it was in pretty bad condition. It had no floor covering, so they carpeted it with a remnant. The right seat in front was broken. It had a wooden block under it, and whenever anyone would try to step out onto the street, it would literally "dump" him out.

One day a couple of George's co-workers at KLO decided they would play a trick on him and "borrow" his car without telling him. He went out, discovered his car was gone and reported the theft to the police. The joke was on them. They scrambled to get his keys back to him and get him to call off the police before they were discovered.

My mother continued helping Father with scheduling and writing copy. He worked hard. (He called it "pounding the pavement.") His accounts grew steadily. He was proving to be a good salesman. "In fact his record was the highest at the radio station, and I have been told that no one has ever topped his record. He had seventy-two accounts on the radio at the same time," Mother wrote proudly.

Father was not the only focus of my mother's loving attention. His paternal grandmother, Amelia, lived in Logan—an hour north by car. Though they did not get to see her very often, my mother called her periodically to check on her. She was in her eighties, and they shared a love for a radio program with a song request line. Amelia's favorite was "The Bells of Saint Mary's," so Mother would call her and tell her to listen to a certain program and hear her song. "That way she would know we loved her and were thinking about her. She really liked that."

Sewing kept my mother happily busy. She saw a pattern in the newspaper for a long christening dress that she thought was very pretty. It had a panel in the front to be embroidered with a "shadow stitching" (worked from the underside) which was in the shape of a tree. Each time a child was to be christened in it, his initials would be embroidered on one of the branches. She wanted to make the dress out of nylon material, but the war in Europe was on. As she shopped for it, she was told that all nylon was being reserved to make parachutes, so she bought white batiste with white organdy for the panel. She lovingly sewed together this gown, along with a little pair of shoes. All nine of her children were christened in this dress. She kept it in her cedar chest all of her life.

She also made white "outing" flannel nightgowns and diapers for the new baby, curtains, aprons, "but not much for myself. One day I saw some pretty lavender material with a black and white leaf pattern. I bought a few yards and a pattern and decided to make myself a maternity dress. I stayed up quite late one night to finish it; then I hung it on the wall at the foot of our bed. The next morning, I told George to look at this pretty new dress that had just cost $4. He looked out of a corner of his eye, then sat up in bed and said, 'What? You bought all that material for only $4. Now that's what I call a bargain!' We had a good laugh. He always made me laugh. His humor is quick and clever. I have always said he would be a good writer for TV shows."

While he had a quick wit, he also had a quick temper. The couple was cleaning the store room one day and Mother had propped the door open with a little dog figurine—about a foot tall. George picked it up and read the inscription on the bottom: "Amapola: My Pretty Little Puppy." It had been given to Olive by an old boy friend, who had won it at a carnival.

"George raised it over his head and smashed it in a million pieces on the cement floor. We were cleaning up chalk for a year. Was this a sign of jealousy? I suppose it was, so I never mentioned ever having a boy friend again—and he was careful not to mention girl friends. We put the past behind us and lived just for each other and our family. (Good advice for newly-weds!)"

In another crackling memory, Mother recalled mopping the floor in the living room. She reached over to move a lamp on a table. Unfortunately she had wet hands and got a bad shock. In fact, she could not let go. "I 'danced' around the living room, yelling some weird sounds. Finally after knocking off a pretty candy dish we had received for a wedding present, I broke the connection and was free from the lamp. I was really shook up!"

I do not know if this shocking event brought on birth spasms, but I do know that my father took my mother on the 18th of October, 1945 to the Dee Hospital in Ogden, Utah to have their first child—me.

Mother was nervous. She had no idea what to expect. She had asked a friend who had given birth the year before what was going to happen. She smiled and said, "Well, it's not what you'd want to do every Sunday afternoon."

At the beginning of the twentieth century, most women gave birth, attended by midwives at home. Occasionally a doctor would be in attendance, but childbirth was recognized as a natural event that occurred in the comfort of a woman's own home, usually with plenty of female friends and family members in attendance. These women compassionately and lovingly supported her during the birth and assisted her with the major transition into motherhood by maintaining her household while the new mother rested, recovered and bonded with her baby, much like my mother's birth in her grandparents' cabin.

By the 1940's, more than eighty percent of all pregnant women gave birth in a hospital in a surgical environment. They were given heavy drugs to disconnect them from the perceptions of pain and put under general anesthesia for the birth of their child.

Mother opted for natural childbirth. Her parents came to check on her, and Vera stayed for awhile to give my father a break. She encouraged her by saying, "Well, the pain can't get much worse—and it's never more than you can stand, so just try to relax and it will soon be over." How happy Vera was to be able to help at this crucial juncture, although she would not be present for the birth, as no family was allowed in the delivery room.

"Mother was always such a comfort to have around when I didn't feel well," Olive wrote. "And not only me. She was always comforting someone. What an angel!"

Except that brief respite, Father stayed right by his wife's side and timed the pains—their frequency and duration—until finally Dr. Ward arrived, checked on her progress and decided Mother was ready to go into the delivery room. Just as they were wheeling her in, the lights went out in the whole hospital.

Somehow my father weaseled his way into the delivery room. She could hear his concerned voice. "Doc," he said, "Maybe I should run home and get my railroad lantern." But the doctor assured him they had a stand-by system and would have lights shortly.

NESTING

"The lights finally came on, and after twenty-three hours of labor, our precious little son, George Virl Jr., was born. (It was now the 19th of October 1945.) When I heard his first cry, I was so excited and thrilled, I cried too. I had never seen such a beautiful baby in my life! He even had his father's cute little nose. As they put me on the gurney to wheel me into my room, they laid him in my arms, and I continued to weep with joy, knowing that George and I had participated in a partnership with God in bringing this miraculous little life into being."

Latter-day Saints believe that life is eternal, and before we come to this earth, we lived as spirit children with our Heavenly Father. Our mortality is a brief moment in that eternity. It is a time of learning, testing, and trial as we meet opposition and make choices that will allow us to prove our worthiness and commitment to God and be reunited with past generations in an unbroken family chain that lasts forever.

Olive wrote, "This dear little bundle lying in my arms was ours to watch over and care for. How I loved him! I was the happiest person in the whole world. There is no joy quite so exquisite as becoming a mother. The twenty-three hours of labor was forgotten instantly."

She thought that Virl was absolutely the most perfect, most intelligent, most beautiful baby in the world. She kept declaring over and over again that she had never been so happy in her life. All the hopes and dreams of womanhood were fulfilled in that single moment. Olive Osmond was a mother.

GEORGE, OLIVE & BABY VIRL

THE DAVIS CABIN WHERE OLIVE WAS BORN

MOUNT PLEASANT HOME

OLIVE'S MATERNAL GRANDPARENTS
Olive Lovenia and Benjamin Nichols

OLIVE'S PATERNAL GRANDPARENTS
Mary Ann and Samuel Watkins Davis

LAVERNA VAN NOY OSMOND

George's Mother

OLIVE'S PARENTS, VERA AND TOM DAVIS

OLIVE – NINETEEN YEARS OLD

OGDEN, UTAH ARMY DEPOT

OLIVE ON HER WAY TO WORK

SERGEANT GEORGE V. OSMOND, AGE 26

GEORGE AND HIS HARLEY

READY FOR A DATE WITH GEORGE

READY TO GO DANCING

HONEYMOON

OLIVE PREGNANT WITH VIRL

GEORGE AND OLIVE – BUSINESS PARTNERS

OLIVE, ALAN, TOM AND VIRL

VIRL, OLIVE, WAYNE, ALAN, GEORGE AND TOM

WAYNE, ALAN, TOM AND VIRL

MERRILL, GEORGE, ALAN, TOM, VIRL,
WAYNE, JAY AND OLIVE

DONNY MAKES SEVEN

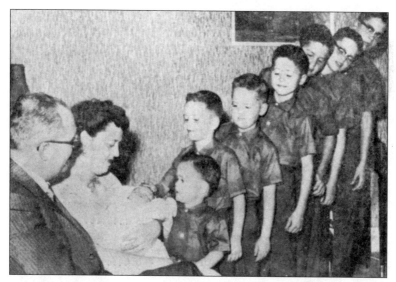

MARIE IS BORN – NEWSPAPER PHOTO

MARIE MAKES EIGHT

GEORGE & BOYS IN OLIVE'S HOMEMADE SHIRTS

THE ANNIVERSARY ORGAN – MUSIC BEGINS

OLIVE TEACHING VIRL AND TOM IN
SCHOOL ROOM

VIRL MILKS THE COW

GEORGE & VIRL ON THE FARM

(TOP) ALAN, TOM AND VIRL
(MIDDLE) JAY, OLIVE, MERRILL, GEORGE, WAYNE
(BOTTOM) MARIE AND DONNY

THE FAMILY IS COMPLETE:
BABY JIMMY IN OLIVE'S LAP

OSMOND BROTHERS, PLUS DONNY

OLIVE WITH HER RECIPE INDEX CARDS

JIMMY MAKES NINE

GEORGE AND OLIVE, THE GOLDEN YEARS

GEORGE WITH VIRL & BABY TOM

CHAPTER NINE

MOTHERHOOD

"I was a nervous mother to say the least, I had no experience to speak of taking care of babies, except my brother, Tommy. I saw the doctors and nurses lifting Virl around, and I said, "Oh, please don't drop him!' I didn't even know how to pick him up properly. I was so afraid of hurting him or kinking his little neck, I would wrap the blanket real tight around him and then pick him up, holding the blanket with both hands—one hand over his chest and one over his knees. It sort of reminded me of a mother cat. I felt pretty weak, so I asked a nurse to walk right by the side of us in case I should faint—I didn't want him to fall. A lady in the room with me—who had just had her fifth child—noticed what I was doing and assured me that babies were not that fragile."

This same woman also answered many, many questions that Olive had about how she took care of those five children. Just like the evening with the Roses, she was filling herself with as much as knowledge as she could. She had decided to have a large family, without consulting George at this point.

When my father felt Mother and baby were all right and getting good care, he told her he had to go out of town for a couple of days. She thought it was for a business meeting of some kind, but when he got back, he had bought her a pair of rhinestone earrings and confessed he had actually been deer hunting. Apparently, becoming a father had overcome him emotionally and he needed to recover. My mother did not find it amusing, however, earrings or not.

After a two-week stay in the hospital (a normal length of time in those days), Mother was so weak when she got home, my father had to carry her into the house. I am certain both were enormously relieved to be together again. They did not like to be separated then and throughout their lives.

"I was extremely nervous about taking care of the baby. One thing that made me quite nervous was Virl had a funny little noise in his throat or in his lungs, and I worried constantly. I put his little bassinet right by my side, so I could hear almost every breath he took."

Mother took me to the doctor twice, but he could not detect any problem. He assured my nervous mother that her son was all right. The problem was that when I was awake and moving around, the doctor could not detect that rattling sound in my chest. It happened only when I was relaxed and asleep. Mother was not convinced. When she took me out of the house, she wrapped me in too many blankets. She was so afraid I would catch a cold.

And because she spent so much time awake at night, she would have no energy to do anything the next day. Father soon caught on to what she was doing, so he bought her a blue platform rocker, so she could rock me to her heart's content. She spent hours a day in it.

She wrote that if I fussed in the night even a little bit, she had a good excuse to get up and take care of me. She would breastfeed me and rock me back to sleep, and then she would read through *Childcraft* and *Parent's Magazine*— "everything I could find to make me be a good mother. Some nights I would read for hours, and then the next morning I was so tired, I could hardly cope." This was in spite of her sweetheart's insistence that she get more rest and do her reading in the daytime.

My father was nervous about handling me, also. He had no experience with babies, at all. He could not even be in the same room when Mother changed diapers or he would throw up!

My mother related a funny experience about Father and me. "One day I left the two of them together and walked up the street to visit my folks. When I came home, there they were—happy as could be—in the corner by the stove. Virl was lying on his bassinet, smiling and enjoying the attention he was getting. George was giving him a back rub with warm olive oil! My poor baby smelled like an Italian salad. But I just laughed. They were, after all, bonding."

Mother wrote about me: "He had big, blue eyes and long, black eyelashes and had such a sweet, shy little spirit. Everybody loved him. I think it was in August when it was announced that there was going to be a "Tomato Days" celebration in Hooper, and there would be a baby contest. People from all over the area were invited to register their babies. Well, of course, I thought I had the cutest baby in the world, so I decided to enter him. George's Mother went with us. I had him dressed in a little red sun suit with a white, mesh front and he did look cute! Sure enough, he walked away with the main prize, 'Little Prince.' I was so excited, I could hardly drive the car home. We went straight to KLO to let his dad know what a charmer he was. His picture was in the newspaper, and we were all so proud of him. Belva made a little crown and scepter for him, and we took lots of pictures." (So that was my one claim to fame. My brothers may have become famous, but none of them was ever crowned a prince!)

Father was very successful in his job at KLO, so my parents decided to buy a new black Dodge (list price $1,389 in 1946) and take a trip. They were pleased to be part of the new post-war, middle class. They decided to travel to Star Valley, Wyoming to see his brother, Rulon, and his family. On the way, they took a shortcut along a side road called "Tin Cup." Mother begged him not to take that road, but he brushed off her concerns and took it anyway. It was early spring, the roads were still muddy, and so they got stuck. It took Father a couple of hours to free the car, while Mother fretted that they would be trapped there overnight in the cold with the baby. He freed them but at the expense of scratches on their new car and a dent in my father's pride.

As he continued to sell more and more accounts, George reached a point where he was making more money than the station manager. When he was informed that they were going to cut back on his wages, he sharply warned them, "You do that, and I'll walk." He had worked so hard and been so diligent at this job, it understandably hurt his pride to suggest that they could not afford to pay him what he earned.

From then on, he was restless, constantly searching for another job. Within a few months, he decided to try his hand at selling real estate. He studied for the tests, took the exam, passed with flying colors and found an opening for a salesman with a man and wife brokerage team. He was their only salesman and very motivated to succeed.

The owners were low-key and easy going. They did not have much of an advertising budget and kept saying things like, "George, don't get excited—maybe you won't make a sale every month, but you'll find out at the end of the year, things average out, and you will have made a pretty good income."

But they did not know my father or my mother, for that matter. The Osmond team turned their attention to building another successful endeavor. Mother could hardly wait to get her hands on the listings and get them organized like she had done with the accounts at the radio station. She also started keeping track of newspaper ads, especially those offered "by owner."

"I would make a list of them each night, and George would call and offer his services if they had any problems in selling homes themselves. Then, in about two weeks, if they were still in the paper, he would make a repeat call. It worked very well. He got a lot of listings that way. I got a big map and with colored pins, pinpointed the various places. For example, red was for residential, blue was for income properties, green was for small farms (over five acres). I also had a card file with details of each listing. It got to be kind of a joke at the office that we had our own multiple listing bureau. Other salesmen would call me when they had to show their client's property—not only from our office but from other offices as well. It was fascinating for me and I enjoyed it."

Father stayed there for a few months, but the pasture looked greener in another office where they had a large sales staff and a larger advertising budget. He thought advertising crucial, so he made another move.

Besides helping her husband, Mother continued to apply her managerial skills to the household. "I kept up on my schedules. I washed clothes Mondays and

Thursdays and tried to have the 'whitest wash in town.' We used our Double-Dexter twin tub washer, which had twin rinse tubs as well. I would run the clothes through two washings and two rinses (added blueing to the last rinse) and was really fussy with the clothes, always washing the white things first, etc. We had no dryers then, so when I hung them out, I would hang all the sheets and pillow cases, the towels, dishtowels, the shirts, the diapers, pants and sox in a very organized pattern (nice to look at if someone drives by. Ha!)."

But, nothing was so engaging or wonderful to Olive as being a mother. "I had never done anything in my life so worthwhile as caring for my son. He was so sweet and had a shy little personality. Motherhood was the ultimate dream as far as I was concerned."

Mother had a protective fierceness when it came to her children. A good example of this was when an insurance salesman who worked with Father's company stayed overnight. I was a toddler by then. The next morning, I was waddling down the hall when "this guy crawled out from the living room on his hands and knees, growling and chasing him. It nearly frightened the wits out of him, and he cried for a long time. I was so angry. I could have mashed that guy!" The poor man could not apologize enough, but Mother would have nothing to do with him. She went into the bedroom with Virl and would not come out until he had left.

The next entry in her journal was August, 1947. She was twenty-two, Dad was thirty. Her parents were staying in Logan where Tom was going to summer school—earning credits toward his master's degree. A phone call came in from the Highway Patrol. The man on the other end wanted to talk to George. Mother heard him say, "Coulee Memorial Hospital," and from the rest of the conversation, she could tell there had been an terrible accident.

"We jumped into our Dodge and dashed north. I called ahead to the hospital and asked for the missionaries to give my parents a blessing of healing. My brother, Tommy, had fortunately emerged unhurt. However, my father was unconscious and in critical condition. His lungs were punctured in several places by broken ribs.

"My mother was conscious and recognized us when we arrived. She expressed relief that we were there and asked us to take care of Daddy first. She had a large bump on her forehead, and her face and arms were cut from broken glass.

"The first thing I did was to call our family physician, Dr. Dumke, in Ogden and ask for him to go up and take personal care for my parents. He stayed up all night with them. He had to keep pumping Daddy's lungs to keep him from drowning in his own blood.

"Later in the day, George and I took Tommy and drove over to the garage where the car had been towed. It was so badly crushed, it was hard to believe any of them got out alive.

From what they could piece together, the family had been coming around a bend in Sardine Canyon—on their way to my parents' house. A big truck came barreling down the canyon on the wrong side of the road. He plowed right into them. There was no way they could have escaped; in fact, if they had been a little farther down the road, they would have gone right over the embankment. Apparently they both threw themselves in front of Tommy to protect him. To make matters worse, the truck driver tried to revive Tom by picking him up and pumping his arms up and down as he tried to get him to walk.

Tom and Vera's recovery was long and difficult. Mother spent many hours each day at their home helping them. But she thanked God every day that their lives had been spared and that the prayers of the elders had been answered.

This happened in August. School started in September, and, although they were not fully recovered, Tom and Vera decided to try to fulfill their duties at the schools they had contracted with. Tom was the Dean of Boys at Davis High School in Kaysville, and Vera taught third grade at Farmington. She took Tommy with her to school there.

The next thing Mother had to cope with was another pregnancy. While still in the first trimester, she became ill with German measles. If that were not enough, I contracted it, too. I had a high fever and was very sick. It was not until later that she was told how dangerous it was to have German measles when expecting a child and the complications it might cause.

To add fuel to the fire, on her next trip to the doctor's office, the doctor checked my mother's blood and found she was RH negative, and that Father was positive. That meant the new baby could develop several complications caused by incompatible blood type and might need a transfusion at birth. Between her parents' accident, the German measles and now the RH factor, it suddenly felt to her that her once-ordered world was beginning to unravel.

But she held onto to her faith, prayed to her Father in Heaven that none of these dire predictions would come true—and He answered her prayers. Their second son, Thomas Rulon Osmond, was born 26 October 1947, a little more than two years after Virl at the same hospital where Mother had previously given birth. He was healthy and strong. The two were so grateful their prayers had been answered. There were no health issues, or so it seemed for the moment.

"I'll never forget the fun we had when we brought him home," Mother wrote. "Virl would walk around and around his little bassinet, and Tommy's pretty little black, beady eyes followed his every move. Virl got such fun out of it. He would walk around opposite directions or look over his head, and Tommy would still follow him.

Bringing my brother home was quite different from when she brought me home. She was a much more confident mother. A few weeks later she wrote, "We had an old rocking chair in the corner of the living room, and one day when I was rocking Tommy, something broke, and it literally dumped us backwards into the corner. I held the baby tight until George came and rescued us. It was really funny." (What a different reaction that was from her concerns for her first baby. After two years of parenting, my mother had become relaxed and self-assured.)

OLIVE OSMOND

OFFICE WORK – OLIVE AND TOMMY DAVIS

CHAPTER TEN

NOMADS

My mother and father had very different personalities and interests. Father's life was hard work and finding new ways of making a better living. He was a negotiator and loved the challenge of putting together business deals. He also liked working in the dirt. For him, fun was hauling hay or driving his tractor on our farm, or working with cattle at his brother's place. My mother used to get so frustrated with him, because nice, clean clothes were not a priority to him. If she did not watch him, he would wear his white business shirt to milk a cow or clean a barn. He never shopped for himself. Mother always sewed or bought his clothes for him. And she always had to go through the closet on laundry day and "find" his dirty clothes, because he would consistently hang them back up. Father thought that clothes should be worn several times before they were dirty enough to wash. Mother thought they should only be worn once. There was nothing pretentious about Father. What you saw was what you got. He was simple and straight-forward in all he did.

But Mother was different. She liked flowers and gardenia soap and spending time at a library or a dress shop. She worked hard too, but her focus was domestic and giving what support she could to Father's business efforts. She was creative and loved to experiment with patterns and recipes. While Father was fairly serious, she was light-hearted and easy-going.

It was this mix that allowed each to fill the needs of the other. Oh, they had their moments when they would clash and disagree. But, on many occasions, Mother said to me, "Marriage is like taking two rough stones and putting them together in a box. If you shake the box back and forth long enough, they rub against each other, knocking off the sharp edges. When they come out, they have taken on a nice polish."

Father was happier in the new real estate office where there was so much activity. He was out checking listings one day and came across a "cute little home" in Riverdale, Utah—just south of Ogden. He wanted Mother to see it, so he dashed home one morning and said, "Let's go—I want to show you something."

Father was never known for doing anything slowly. When he said, "Jump," one jumped. He would always walk ten paces ahead of anyone he was walking with, including Mother. No one could work fast enough to suit him. So, when it came to finishing her dream house (which at that point, was only a basement), and Father got another idea in his head, that was that. There was no changing his mind, no turning back.

So Mother was introduced to a cute white house that sat on top of a hill overlooking the valley. "There was a lovely, big raspberry patch, something I had always wanted," Olive wrote. "The honeysuckle made the yard smell heavenly, and there were climbing roses everywhere. It was so beautiful! A big weeping willow tree stood near the back door. The front yard sloped down to a white fence and gate that had pretty purple clematis growing over the top of it. The yard was filled with wild flowers—poppies, bachelor buttons, and lots of others I couldn't even identify."

She fell in love with it. The house was vacant so they could move right in, which they did. They found a buyer for their basement house and property on Wall Avenue and were soon relocated and settled.

They both enjoyed their time in this little house. Mother wrote, "George took over a basement den where, on a maroon-colored felt wallboard, he mounted his collection of coins and a knife he had made from a spent bullets he had saved from his war days in England.

"I got a lot of pleasure from our raspberry patch. We had all we wanted to eat fresh, and I bottled some almost every day. Each morning I would get up early and pick them before the sun got hot. I bottled dozens of quarts and made a lot of jam.

"But just when I was feeling settled and cozy, George came home and announced we would be moving—again—this time to Cedar City in southern Utah. He had been offered a good position in an already established insurance agency. The owner was retiring, so George would be able to buy the agency. (There was a clause that the owner could come back, but George felt it was doubtful that he would.)

I loved our little white house that we were in, with all its trees and flowers and raspberries. It was hard for me to even think of leaving it. But what could I do? I knew I loved George more than that house and I wanted him to be successful, so I consented and followed him."

They sold their Riverdale home to my grandparents, which comforted Mother somewhat knowing someone she loved got the house. They packed some of their belongings in a trailer and headed about five hours south. My brother, Tommy, was only a few weeks old at the time. "I wasn't feeling a bit strong, and it was sad leaving my folks. My mother was especially unhappy to see us go. I think I know how the Mormon pioneers must have felt when the Prophet Brigham Young would call families to leave their settled homes in the Salt Lake Valley and migrate to new areas in the state and establish communities there. We left our possessions behind in storage and off we went."

They landed in a furnished apartment at the Cedar Crest Lodge, paying $80 per month, which was expensive. Being as frugal as they were, they planned to only be there temporarily.

Olive moved continually in her youth from Samaria to Thatcher and back, so I imagine that the moving was not as disruptive as it might have been had she just lived in one place for all of her childhood. Father was making enough money at this point that she did not have to work, but she had two boys under the age of two to care for, and anyone who says that is not work, has not raised kids!

"I decided to be a good manager/housekeeper so I set up a schedule just as though I were running a business. It went something like this:

Sunday: Attend Church meetings. Study scriptures and read good Church books. Prepare a simple dinner (actually prepared the day before).

Monday: Wash day and bedroom day. Change sheets on beds. Dust and clean bedroom. Take all soiled clothes from closet. Clean drawers in dresser. (This way they would be clean and ready for new, freshly laundered clothes.) Wash clothes and hang to dry. Gather and dampen any that needed ironing. Roll dampened clothes.

Tuesday: Ironing day and bathroom day. Clean bathroom thoroughly; also clean mirrors, windows, wipe figurines and dust thoroughly. Iron clothes. Set aside any That needed mending.

Wednesday: Mending and sewing day. Also living room day. This day I did any mending, sewing on buttons etc. that needed to be done on clothes. I also cleaned the living room thoroughly, arranged books in shelves, vacuumed, and dusted. If I had plenty of time—while the sewing machine was out—I would sew (mostly shirts for the boys and dresses or aprons for me).

Thursday: My day off! I looked forward to this day. It was sort of a reward for having things in order. Sometimes I would just spend extra time with my little boys. Or I would read—or sew (perhaps finish some project started Wednesday). Once in awhile George would come home and stay with the boys, and I would do some shopping or go to the library. It was a leisure day.

Friday: Kitchen day. Grocery shopping. Refrigerator and cupboards were cleaned thoroughly (so they would be ready for new groceries). Floor was mopped and waxed.

Saturday: Baking day and food preparation. Usually I would cook a roast, make a salad, set Jello, bake bread, bake a cake or cookies, etc. so I would not have to prepare anything on Sunday, the Sabbath.

Mother always kept a daily schedule, so we as a family knew exactly how to spend our time. She kept it flexible, but it surely kept us on our toes, and things ran smoothly with our big family.

They had not lived there long until Mother noticed a funny little "rattling" sound in Tommy's chest that I once had. This set off the intense worry that she had with me. She decided that they should take him back to Ogden and have an X-ray taken by the same doctor I had.

They decided they were paying too much rent for the furnished apartment, so Father made arrangements for an unfurnished one in the same court. They would go to Ogden, take Tommy and me to the doctor, and get the trailer and furniture they had left in Riverdale.

At the appointment, the doctor ordered X-ray treatments for an enlarged thymus gland in both of us. During the three trips back to Ogden for these doctor visits, Mother was torn. "I thought we were doing the right thing, but I'll never forget the horrible feeling I had when Tommy took one of the treatments. Just as they turned on the X-ray, his little hand reached up and knocked the machine so that his right ear got the X-ray. I felt like grabbing him and running with him. I wanted to scream. I just 'knew' something had gone wrong. I cried and was miserable for days over it. (I was assured that it would do him no harm, but I was not convinced.)"

On one trip back home to Cedar City, they came around a bend in the highway—the roads slick with ice and snow—and met a big Greyhound bus sliding toward them. Father yanked the steering wheel as far to the right as he could, and the back end of the bus barely missed them. (I am certain her parents' accident must have flashed through her mind.) "I thought for sure we were going to be smashed and quickly threw myself over Virl and Tom to protect them. But the Lord was with us, and we escaped tragedy. I was so upset over that one, I cried for an hour."

Believe it or not, in a short time they moved out of the unfurnished apartment and bought a 27-foot trailer house at a near by trailer court. The trailer was smaller than their apartment. Mother said, "We worked to squeeze our possessions into that little trailer. Some things we sold. What was left we packed into the car, and George drove me and the boys to the trailer. There were so many of our items in the car, there was barely enough room for the four of us to ride in it. He left the car there for me to unpack, and he walked off to work. Over his shoulder, he called out, "Good luck. I'll be back at noon."

Mother put Tommy in his little silver walker, and I took charge of entertaining him, while Mother made the numerous trips from the car into the trailer, putting things away. She was thrilled with the little mobile home, but I think she taught herself to like any situation she found herself in.

She could hardly believe there was so much room—closets, drawers and cubby holes. There was a "place for everything!" By noon, when Father got home, he could hardly believe his eyes that everything was already put away and out of sight. Like all the other places they had lived in, Mother set about to make a house a home.

However, they began to be disenchanted with Cedar City. The wind was always blowing with garbage cans rolling down the street. For some reason, the couple had a hard time making any close friends there, and besides, they missed seeing their extended family in Ogden on a regular basis.

But the straw that broke the camel's back for my father was that the man who was going to sell Father his interest in the insurance agency decided to come back into the business. He wanted my father to do the "leg work," and he would manage the office. But that offer was not why Father had moved to Cedar City. He was determined to have his *own* business, so my nomadic parents made another move back home to Ogden to start their own real estate and insurance agency.

They had the trailer pulled back up to Ogden and parked it in Grandma LaVerna's backyard for the time being. This was the same house where Mother and her parents had once lived when she was single and worked at the Adjutant General's office. Her parents had sold it to LaVerna after Mother and Father were married. They kept it in the family, if for no other reason, than for a sentimental one.

My father found a piece of property for his office in an area that was called Five Points in Ogden and immediately hired a contractor to start building. As soon as it was finished, they moved their trailer right in the back of the building (the sixth move in one year), so Mother could take care of her two little boys and be close enough to do the office work.

But she did not seem to mind all the changes. She wrote in her journal: "Our first account was a florist and gradually we built up a successful little enterprise. We called it the Five Points Agency.

"I designed calling cards for George. They said, 'If you're sick, see your doctor; if you need legal advice, see your lawyer; but if you need insurance, see George V. Osmond.'

"I also ordered little pink, blue and yellow baby rattles and kept track of the new babies being born in the newspaper and would send the parents a 'congratulations' card, and a rattle with attached advertising."

One day a man came to the office looking for a typist to type up contracts and letters for him. He was selling oil stock. Mother thought that might be a good way to make some extra money. He was to pay her per page.

She kept carbon copies of the things she had worked on, so she would have an accurate count of the number of pages, when he paid her. Time went on—no money. The flies grew, and finally she asked if he would mind paying her.

He said, "Well, you haven't done much yet." She showed him the file of documents. He was quite surprised and offered to pay her with oil stock.

"I didn't think that was a bad idea—lots of people were buying it, so I agreed. It turned out to be worthless."

In the spring of 1949, a couple came into the office to list their house. They wanted to sell it and buy a trailer home. My enterprising father showed them his trailer, and immediately they wanted to trade the trailer for the equity in their house. My parents told them they would think about it, which they did—for about forty-eight hours.

The house they bought was quite dirty and needed a great deal of repair. The location was not that great either—it was clear across town—which meant Father would have to do a lot of commuting. The thing that really sold them was the big, fenced backyard where Tommy and I could safely run and play to our hearts' content. "I can still see Virl driving the tricycle with Tom standing on the back with his arms around Virl as they rode around and around the yard." Father built a big sand box on the south side of the house and filled it with clean sand. We spent many hours there.

Mother wrote, "We stripped, painted, repaired and furnished our new house. Like all our other moves, our work and organization was a labor of love and sharing and dreams. During this time, George won a course of study from the International Correspondence School at this time. Actually there were three courses he was able to take: Business math, advertising and one other—I cannot remember. We bought our first wire recorder and during the day I would record the lessons for George. Then at night, after dinner, he would lie down on the couch and we would listen to the lessons, try to figure out the answers to the questions and then send them in. It was fun, and we both learned a lot."

Many years later, as my parents looked back on this year of moves and changes, they realized just how much it worked to prepare them for the many moves they would embark upon as their children entered into show business. My mother would say, "No matter how difficult a test may be, never ask the Lord, 'Why?' Only ask Him, 'What am I supposed to learn from this?' There is a purpose in all things that happen to us, whether by our own choice or as a consequence of the choices of others. The trick is to realize that and to build upon it." My mother was a very wise woman.

OLIVE OSMOND

WAYNE, VIRL, ALAN, OLIVE, BABY MERRILL, TOM

CHAPTER ELEVEN

THE EARLY 50's

Whenever I read through my mother's journals, it seems that just as her life appeared settled and running smoothly, something happened to disrupt it. But then, I guess, such is the nature of life. It seems she learned to enjoy the quiet times and renew her mental, physical and emotional strength, so she had the reserves she needed for those inevitable challenges that came up. Tom and I turned out to be one very big challenge.

Mother recorded in her journal: "The sandbox was just underneath Virl's and Tommy's bedroom window, so I would go in there and look outside to check on them quite often. One day I knocked at the window to let them know I was watching over them. I noticed that Virl was the only one that looked up. Then he would reach over, touch Tom and point to me in the window. They would both smile and then go back to their playing. It bothered me, so I went back a second, third and fourth time to see if they did the same thing.

Each time, Virl would always have to let Tom know I was knocking."

My mother's mind spun as she tried to think back and remember if there were other times that Tom and I seemed unaware of the sounds around us.

"Virl had been very slow in learning to talk, and his words were not really clear. He seemed to skip saying the 'r's' and 's's' in his words. Then I recalled times when I would try to tell either of the boys to do something. Virl would stare at me the longest time before responding. Many times I had to 'show' him what I meant. Tom seemed always distracted and uninterested in things I said to him. If I tried to instruct him, it was always Virl who finally seemed to make eye contact with Tom and get the message through. So I called George at work and talked to him about it. We decided we had better take them to the doctor for a hearing test. We knew there was a School for the Deaf in Ogden, so I called them and told them my concerns and arranged for an appointment."

My parents felt a great deal of anxiety as they drove to the meeting with the audiologist at the school. Mother said it was as though there was a hole in her stomach. She wanted them to tell her that her sons were fine and not to worry, but deep inside she knew there was something wrong. She remembered the German measles she had when she was pregnant with Tom and how I had been sick with them, too. And there were those X-ray treatments that we had for our so-called enlarged thymus condition. Waves of guilt filled her as she struggled to dismiss a sense of heartache rising up within her that perhaps *she* had been responsible for what had happened to us.

When the tests were concluded, my parents were told that both their boys had severe hearing losses. Mine was diagnosed as about a 75% decibel loss, and Tom had an 87% decibel loss. Dr. Nelson, a specialist at the deaf school then shocked my parents when he told them, "You might as well get used to the fact that your two boys will have to spend the rest of their lives in an institution."

"What a cold, frightening feeling came over us!" she wrote. "We were in a state of shock for days. Not our boys! The tests must be wrong. They were so healthy when they were born—it's a mistake!"

Mother prayed and prayed to God for comfort— for a miracle. She held her little sons in her arms and just wept. After a few days of agony and distress over this unwanted news, they came together and did what they had always done when life challenged them.

"We felt that we just could not turn our sweet little boys over to an institution," she wrote. "We loved them too much. They were our little sons and whatever they needed to learn to function and participate in life we would be the ones to teach it to them.

"I began reading everything I could get my hands on about the deaf world—how difficult it was to teach the speech and hearing impaired to talk and how frustrated the large majority of deaf people were when trying to cope in a hearing world. And then there was this controversy over whether the deaf should even be taught to speak at all! One camp championed only teaching them speech, and another said they should only learn how to use sign language. Still a third said that they needed both. There was actually a culture among the deaf themselves that developed due to their sense of isolation and limitation in a hearing world. I needed to talk to my sons and they needed to talk to me. We needed language and communication."

So my parents determined not to institutionalize us. They sent us to classes at the deaf school but brought us home at night. At the school, sign language was stressed, but at home we learned how to talk.

"I had heard of the John Tracy Clinic in Los Angeles," she recorded, "so I wrote to them and got what literature they had. It wasn't as helpful as I had hoped, but I was encouraged by the positive stories about the achievements of other deaf people in the world. I had lived with teachers all my life (my own father and mother), and they offered to help me organize a special learning curriculum for Virl and Tom."

And thus began my mother's life-long commitment to helping not only us in our individual struggles with being hearing impaired, but also in studying and supporting medical research in the area of deafness. In later years, her efforts led to the establishment of the Osmond Foundation. It helped to provide medical help and hearing aids for many deaf children. The success of this foundation led to an expansion in their desire to help all children with medical and physical disabilities and needs. Eventually the Children's Miracle Network was born. It has raised millions of dollars for children's hospitals in the United States and all over the world.

Today, the Ogden School for the Deaf offers individually designed instruction in sign language development, auditory verbal training, daily living skills, vocational skills, assistive adaptive technology training, deaf culture and computer technology. But when my parents and grandparents were trying to help us, they did not even have the rudiments of American Sign Language to work with.

"We prayed for guidance," my mother wrote, "and really believed we were guided in our decisions and in the way we needed to handle the training of our sons. First we came to grips with the 'Why us?' question. Instead, we turned it around and said, 'Why not us?' Who were we that God would trust us with these two special little boys?' God never gives anyone more than they can handle. So our training began."

When my parents found out Tom and I were deaf, Mother was several months pregnant with her third child. She talked to her doctor about it, and he actually tried to discourage her from having any more children. He suggested that because their first two children were deaf, all their children might be born deaf.

Then, on June 22, 1949, Mother gave birth to her third son, Alan Ralph Osmond, at Dee Hospital, where his other brothers were born. My parents immediately began to worry that he too might be hearing impaired. Fortunately, tests proved that their worries were unfounded. Alan came as a healthy little boy. However, he did not arrive without his share of tension in the delivery room.

"I had a peculiar experience when Alan was born," Mother recorded. "Perhaps I was just partially unconscious, but when I read about people having 'out of body experiences,' it makes me wonder if I weren't pretty close to that myself.

"I could hear the doctor and nurses talking, when one of the nurses became quite excited and called the doctor to come quickly. She said my blood pressure was dropping and I wasn't responding to her when she tried to wake me. I sensed nothing, but I felt like I was floating up to the ceiling—I wasn't aware of even having a body. There was no pain and I felt like a slowly blinking light (which was probably my heart beating). The doctor called my name, but I didn't try to answer. He called me again just a little louder and I thought, 'I wish they would just leave me alone.' The third time he called, I finally responded. I woke up and found a nurse was slapping my face. It turns out that I was reacting to a loss of blood."

We became a very busy family in 1951. My father grew tired of commuting across town to the office, so my parents decided to rent their house and moved into yet another small home on Third Street, where they immediately began cleaning, remodeling and upgrading it as they had with all the others.

With three little boys, keeping house, and the office work, Mother was kept quite busy. She loved the convenience of living in a place behind the office. It was close to the church, close to the grocery stores, and again they were close to her parents, who lived a couple of blocks away. They were also close to George's mother, who lived about four blocks down the street.

THE EARLY 50's

My parents served in a number of volunteer positions in the church ward (congregation) they lived in. In the Church of Jesus Christ of Latter-day Saints, (the Mormons) the entire membership serve in "callings." These are unpaid lay positions, from Sunday school teachers to bishops and scouting leadership.

In this particular ward, Father was called as a Scoutmaster, and Mother was called to teach the Book of Mormon class in the Relief Society, the church women's organization, which was established by the Prophet Joseph Smith in 1830 as a charity and service organization run entirely by the women in the church.

Father spent many hours with the Scouting program, teaching, taking the boys on camping trips and to various activities. (The Mormon Church is an ardent supporter of the Scouting program, offering church resources and facilities for boys to work on merit badges, learn survival skills and learn by precept and example to honor the Scouting moral code.)

Mother was a natural teacher. She loved to study the scriptures and enjoyed an excuse to learn and instruct. The Relief Society is a boon to the women of the church. There, friendships are developed. They serve and help one another and share their experiences in all the domestic responsibilities to better their homes and their lives.

Father was also very busy with his the real estate and insurance business, which was growing exponentially. He arranged for appointments with potential clients nearly every day, so he could sell more insurance policies. He also had many potential home buyers which he would take to see the various real estate properties he had listed for sale.

"I remember one day he came home so excited about a deal," she wrote. "He had sold a health insurance package for the Ogden City employees. He met with some pretty tough competition but he had won the contract! That sale really helped our income."

In one of the service callings that Father had in the church, he was working with minority groups in the area, such as Native Americans, helping the economically disadvantaged to find employment. One day he came home and announced he had hired a Native American woman to help Mother with the housework and the boys.

"I wasn't too thrilled with the idea," she wrote, "but I knew I needed someone. When I met Virginia Menard, I knew George must have been inspired. She was so sweet and pleasant. She worked hard and kept everything so clean and neat! We got to be just like sisters, and she really was a lot of help to me. She loved to embroider and put little designs on all the nightgowns

I made for baby number four." (Yes, there was another Osmond boy on the way.)

Between running an insurance agency and a real estate agency and caring for three and a half sons—two of which needed special training, my parents were very busy people. But their extended family reached out and gave them extensive support.

"They would come over often and bring us treats—everything from cooked roasts and casseroles to hot bread, butter, oranges, apples etc. We often laughed about their tactics of "stealing" our dirty clothes when we weren't looking and bringing them back the next day all washed and ironed. They were so sweet. We loved them so much!"

Believe it or not, Mother had never had a baby shower for any of her pregnancies. She felt a little uneasy about finally having one for her fourth child and having people bring her gifts. "I never had a birthday party when I was growing up. We were quite poor, and my parents just could not afford to give me one. Also they did not feel right asking others to bring me gifts, when they too were struggling under the hard economic times of the day. I understood their way of thinking."

But she did not have much to say about this shower. Friends planned it, and they, plus family, filled the house on the appointed day. She was given several baby *girl* dresses at the party. Everyone thought, since she had had three boys, she was sure to get a girl this time. But as destiny would have it, the bass of the family was born instead, and the dresses were lovingly packed away in a trunk for a future day.

"On August 28, 1951 our dear little son, Melvin Wayne Osmond was born at the Thomas Dee Hospital in Ogden, Utah. He weighed 7 lbs. 3 oz. and had a different look from the other three boys. He had this cute little round face, and I was delighted that he actually looked like me. My childhood pictures surely proved that. To our relief, he was healthy and strong and most importantly, he could hear.

"Our housekeeper, Virginia, hovered over him and carried him whenever and wherever she got a chance. When we went to church, if he made the slightest cry, she would walk him to the back of the chapel and quietly 'dance' with him. As he grew older, she would let him pull on her red, dangling, pierced earrings—which almost made me shiver. I was sure he was going to pull them right out!"

We introduced Virginia to the teachings of the Mormon Church while she lived with us. She eventually chose to be baptized and was an enthusiastic convert, devoted to keeping the commandments. In a church priesthood blessing she received some time later,

Virginia was promised that she would be a missionary to her own people. She said to me, 'How can that be? My people are very few (Assiniboine tribe), and they live clear up in Montana!'"

Most of the Assiniboine tribe lives on a reservation in Fort Peck, which is in the northeast corner of Montana. Once 10,000 strong in the 1780's, they now only numbered 2800 members on their reservation. The Assiniboine's had been roving buffalo hunters who fought and hunted on horseback. Like other Plains Indians, they had lived in teepees and had a proud heritage of independence and self-sufficiency. They cared for and honored the land they dwelled on and considered it sacred. They respected all living creatures and only used what was needed and maintained a simple nomadic life.

After being confined to a reservation, they struggled to hold on to their sense of culture. At that time, they had a 76 percent unemployment rate. Their confined existence and loss of purpose as a people created a high alcoholism and drug use rate also. So Virginia's response to her blessing was understandable.

About a year later some people that owned a store in the area needed a housekeeper and could pay her well, so Virginia moved in with them. She then met a man named Wesley Firemoon, and they married and moved to Montana. Later she wrote to the Osmond's from a hospital where she was being treated for some serious health problems. At the end of her letter, she said, "I thought you would like to know that since I married Wesley, every member of his family has joined the Church." What a fulfillment of a blessing!

"Not long after that, Wesley wrote us a sad letter telling us of her passing and how much he loved her. She had been a part of our family for a short period of time, but she will always be in my heart forever."

So the family continued to grow, and soon it was time for Tom and me to attend school. "We finally sent Virl to kindergarten at a school about two blocks away instead of sending him to the school for the deaf. We got him a new hearing aid which he was not too fond of, but it helped him hear well enough that we felt he could probably function in a classroom with other hearing children. However, his hearing aid was not the discreet behind-the-ear type they have today. It had wires that came down to a big black box he had to wear strapped to his chest. It was big and bulky and very noticeable. But that was the only kind available at that time. Some children in his class were cruel, and they pulled the hearing aids out of his ears and made fun of him.

"Virl didn't say or do much about the taunting—in fact he didn't even mention it to us at home. He just 'suffered in silence' until one day, one of his tormenters went a step too far. He started pushing Virl around, so Virl smacked him a good one and broke his own little finger in the process. The bully backed off and Virl was not tormented again because he wore a hearing aid."

In her research, Mother had heard that the Maico Company had manufactured a 'Train-Ear' unit that was considered helpful in teaching the hearing impaired, so she ordered one.

It was a combination—record player, microphone and earphones. There was a compression unit in the ear phones, so you could turn it very loud, but there was no danger of damaging the nerves. A book came with it with pictures of various things that made sounds—a bear, a cow, a dog, a vacuum cleaner, a car, and an airplane and so on. I remember how Tom and I loved to hear the bear growl, and we also loved that microphone. We would take turns putting on the headset and making different sounds into the microphone. When we could not hear a word or a letter, we did not know what kind of a sound it made, so we could not duplicate it in speech. This machine helped us form words and sounds correctly.

Mother wrote: "I set aside time every day for a 'home school' with Virl and Tom. I tried to create a fun atmosphere for learning how to speak, something that was exciting for them. With the microphone I could talk to them, and they could use what residual hearing they had to repeat back what they thought they heard, turning the volume up or down as needed.

"Before we had that machine, communication with Virl and Tom had been so difficult. They would struggle to say things but their speech was garbled and hard to understand. Especially little Tom's. I remember one heartbreaking time when Tommy was sick and he could not make me understand what was wrong. I thought he was hungry or something. Finally, Tommy collapsed down onto the floor and started beating his fists on the ground, because he could not get through to me. He was so frustrated. I sat down on the floor and pulled him into my lap and we both cried. It was only then that I felt the fever on his forehead and understood what he was trying to get through to me."

School at home became so much fun that Alan and Wayne wanted to join in, too, so my parents decided to build a small school room onto the west side of the house. Father plastered one whole wall and then painted it with blackboard paint and put a chalk ledge along the bottom. They could now write letters and draw pictures to their heart's content. He built shelves, so they could keep their books and toys separate, too.

"We chose colors for each one—Virl (blue), Tom (red), Alan (yellow) and Wayne (orange) and painted their shelves those colors. We also painted the chairs and one leg of the table in each of those colors. It was a delightful place, and I loved spending time teaching all of them," Mother wrote. Those same colors they had assigned to each boy became the dominant colors on their costumes as they performed on stage later.

Besides her home schooling duties, Mother still worked with Father in the business and had numerous conversations with clients. So she decided she should get her own real estate license, which she studied for and received. Not many women were real estate agents in those days. But my mother wasn't just any woman!

One day an elderly lady came to the office looking for an investment. Father had been told that this woman had looked at property with every salesman in town and probably was not really serious about buying anything. So he sort of shuffled her off to Mother and asked her to take the time to find something for her. She took on the challenge.

"I showed her nearly everything that was available. There was one large brick house on the east bench that she liked quite well. I said, 'Do you know what I would do if I owned that house? I would divide it and make two apartments out of it—one to rent out and one to live in for myself. She liked the idea so well that we came back to the office and she bought it! Everyone was surprised. I turned it over to George to do the paper work, because I had something a little more important to do.

"I dashed home, grabbed my suitcase, which was already packed, and George took me to the hospital. On the 30th of April 1953, our little blond son, Merrill Davis Osmond, joined our family. What a treasure he was! Now we had five little boys—the joy of my life!"

Merrill was born at the end of the month when Mother normally sent out statements for their insurance accounts. So she had just tucked the records into her suitcase, along with some statement forms, envelopes and stamps, and brought them to the hospital with her. On the 4th of May (her birthday), the doctor came in and saw her working on them. He laughed and said, "My goodness, child, if you're needed that badly at home. I'd better sign your release!"

"I remember vividly riding home in the car," she recalled, "and looking at my new baby's face and telling George what a precious little spirit I thought he was. He had this kind, sweet disposition. He hardly ever cried. In fact, my mother said to me one day, 'Now don't you neglect him just because he's so good!'"

No one could fault Olive's mothering. She was amazingly patient and kind and intuitive with her little group of boys. But she was human. She wrote: "I don't remember giving any of the children a real spanking — maybe a little 'love tap' once in awhile when they were really mischievous. But I do remember one day being extra-tired and frustrated and out of patience, and I gave Alan one of those 'love taps' for something he had done. He looked up at me with tears in his big brown eyes. He did not say a word but his looks did. It was as though he was saying, 'Mother, what in the world have I done so terrible that you would treat me like this?'

"The crushed countenance in that broken-hearted dear little face pained me. I felt absolutely awful and vowed I would never spank any of my children again, and I do not believe I ever did. All I could think of was what choice little spirits I had around me and how grateful I was to be their mother."

On Christmas Day my parents always had "smorgasbord" and invited relatives and friends to stop by for dinner. This tradition began when they took their first trip to California, where one of father's relatives took them to a restaurant called, "Hit 'O Sweden." There they ate from a huge smorgasbord or buffet of serving dishes that were overflowing with good food.

"There was so much food and in such variety that you could not possibly sample it all," Mother said. "It was displayed so beautifully, too. That it made a lasting impression on me and from then on, we had our own smorgasbord at Christmas time—everything from molded gelatin salads to hot rolls, casseroles, etc."

This tradition was happily carried on in our home for decades; even after all of us boys were married and having families of our own. We all had our favorite salads that Mother would make for us on our birthday, but on Christmas she would make all nine! They were called Virl's salad, Tom's salad, etc. There was always a big turkey (except for one year when we had a big goose that Father got from his brother. We joked that Mother had to cook the goose or her goose would be cooked!)

We had stuffing and gravy and yams and at least three different kinds of vegetables, homemade bread and rolls and jam. And there was Grandma Davis' famous lemon meringue pie, along with pumpkin pie and Grandma Osmond's mixed-berry pie and frozen raspberry jam. Father made hot apple cider, and the smell wonderfully filled the house with the scents of cinnamon and spices. There were Christmas cookies and ice cream, too. Mother always decorated the table with a holiday tablecloth and candles.

When we sat around that bountiful feast, and bowed our heads in prayer and thanks, we all held hands and soaked in the love and warmth that filled our hearts. Ask any of my siblings what they got on any given Christmas, and they probably will not remember. But ask them about Mother's Christmas smorgasbord, and their mouths still water.

"One couple always came to visit us on the holidays," wrote Mother. "The wife said, 'Well, you have five children now—I hope you're not planning to have any more!' (Merrill was about eight months old at that time). "I was really offended by that, so I asked, 'Why not? I've always wanted a big family.'"

She said, 'Well, I've had experience. I came from a big family, and it was a nightmare! I never remember coming home from school that there was not a big batch of dishes waiting for me to do or a big batch of diapers to wash. One of the kids always needed a haircut—or their shoes were worn out—or their clothes needed ironing—someone always looked 'tacky.' With a big family there's just no way to keep up on things. There's no privacy, no peace and quiet, and there is never enough money. You just can't spread yourself that thin and do a good job!"

"Well, I knew she was wrong. She had to be!" Mother wrote. "As soon as they left, I told George what she had said. Then I said, 'Let's work out a system. No one is ever going to say anything like that about *our* kids." So they evaluated their system of organizing and caring for their boys and made some adjustments. Father gave them all a haircut every Saturday. He also made sure their shoes were polished for church. Also on Saturday night, Mother pressed all of the clothes and made sure things were ready for Sunday, which was their first priority.

Mother wrote: "I told my mother, Vera, what the visitor had said to me and how we felt about it. She volunteered to take over the project of keeping their little jeans patched. She bought new, dark denim cloth and when the knees in their jeans started wearing, she would put the same size patch on both knees. These weren't their school jeans, though. When they came home, they changed from their good school jeans to their patched play jeans, and they always looked so neat."

My mother learned to sew shirts and began making them in sets. She wrote that the boys loved dressing alike (but I remember being a bit embarrassed by our uniformity). "When I caught on to the art of making them (along with the buttonholes), there was no stopping me. I would buy the Dan River plaids—every color of the rainbow. They had such pretty, small plaids—so appropriate for boys' shirts.

"It was a challenge, but it was rewarding," she wrote. "People would remark how nice they always looked when we took the boys out to meetings and even shopping. My real 'pay day' came at a parent/teacher meeting. Two of their teachers came up to me and said, 'We just want you to know what a pleasure it is to have your children in our classes. Not only are they well-mannered, but they always are so neat and clean.'"

Once my parents organized the physical care of us children, they looked at how they could better influence our discipline and behavior. Father was a strong advocate of hard work. It was okay for his boys to have play time, but he felt they needed to learn responsibility, too, so he established a chore chart of duties suited to the ages of each child. He took this very seriously and would come home from work each day, and first thing, he would ask if we had done our chores. As we grew older, I believe that my father purposely bought a small farm just to keep us busy!

As the oldest, I got stuck with milking our old cow, Pansy, twice a day. I got switched in the face by her tail more times that I care to count. I had to get up at five every morning to milk her before school, and then again after school. That chore was a thorn in my side for many years. But there was no denying that the hard work taught us many lessons and increased our skills, productivity and even self-esteem.

Our homes were always small. No one had their own bedroom. Father introduced military discipline and built a dormitory behind the kitchen on our farm. It was lined with beds on one wall and cubby holes, shelves and drawers on the other. Every time Mother had a baby, another bed was added.

Then my parents looked at our spiritual welfare, and my mother decided that we needed to have one special night a week—a family night—where she would make a special dinner with a special dessert, and she and Father would pick a gospel subject to teach us. We would read from the scriptures and sing songs. And Mother would play on her small organ. (Monday night today is designated in the Mormon church as "family home evening night," and families do exactly the same thing worldwide.)

So this was how my parents decided to manage their large family. It was the discipline and organization that kept our family together and also prepared the boys for the discipline that they would need when they embarked on their musical career.

228 WASHINGTON BLVD

CHAPTER TWELVE

TWO TWENTY-EIGHT

Father was always out looking for additional properties to list with his real estate company. One day he came across an older brick home that was on two acres of land. He had been thinking for some time about his need for a larger home. He had five sons, and his wife was pregnant again. They definitely were in need of more room. He came home quite enthused about the idea of buying this particular house.

He said to Mother, "Olive, get your coat and come with me. I've just found the best deal in town!"

My mother gave him a questioning look. They had just finished remodeling their current home. She was in the first trimester of her sixth pregnancy and was not feeling all that well. She knew if she got into that car with Father, he was going to try to sell her on another house, and she was not so sure she was ready for that again. But she had learned that, when he said, "Come now!" there was no arguing with him. She had to go. So they herded the kids in the car and went to 228 North Washington Boulevard, in Ogden.

At first blush, it looked like just another old home, badly in need of repairs. It did not even have enough bedrooms to take care of their current needs. But it did have two acres of land and a big orchard, which really attracted Father. It also had a nice fireplace in the front room which was something they had never had before, and that pleased Mother.

Although it was smaller than they needed instead of larger, they could see its potential. It was also empty, so they could have immediate possession if they wanted it. And then there were the boys, who jumped out of the car and disappeared into the orchard and barn to explore and play. They bought it on the spot.

Now they needed to make a decision whether to move to the new house before Christmas or move in after. If they stayed where they were, they could enjoy the new carpet and the newly decorated house and school room they had just worked so hard to fix up. Or they could move now and enjoy...a fireplace. The new house just had too many issues that needed to be resolved, so they chose to stay and have their traditional Christmas smorgasbord in their current home.

They called the new house, "Two twenty-eight." Father did not even wait to move in before he bought a cow and some chickens. He plowed and prepared a garden spot for spring planting and planted more fruit trees than the considerable number of existing apple, peach and apricot trees. Those trees had not been pruned for several years, so he tore into that project, too. He then bought an additional piece of ground next to the house which had boysenberries growing on it.

"Now we had a real farm," Mother wrote. "There were so many things to be done. The house was a sturdy old brick place, but it was quite run-down.

"We had a living room, dining room, kitchen, bath, three small bedrooms, a closed-in back porch and a half-basement for storage. We really needed more room and planned to build on later. But with some old army bunk beds, we stuffed all the boys in one room, put George and me in another, and made the third room into a nursery. We were as cozy as seven bugs in a rug!"

My parents were not afraid to tackle almost any remodeling project by this time, so they were ready to start on this one. The first thing they needed to do was remove the obtrusive brick chimney attached to the big, old coal stove in the kitchen. "It jutted out from the wall both in the kitchen and the adjoining dining room. It took up too much space. So brick by brick we knocked it down and had the older boys, Virl and Tom, carry the bricks out to the back lot. By the time the boys were finished helping, they were covered in soot. It took two baths to get it all off of them, and then I had to clean all the black soot out of the tub!"

As usual, they scrubbed and cleaned, painted woodwork and papered walls, washed windows and hung new curtains. Soon the place was "sparkling."

"We bought a green rug for the dining room floor." (Mother loved the color green and followed that theme in many homes, painting the walls a soft pale green color. She said it was very relaxing for her.) "I cannot think about that rug without remembering little Wayne, who was three years old at the time, coming in from the kitchen doing a little shuffle with one foot. We started clapping and praising him for his unique dance. He looked at us casually, shrugged his shoulders and said, 'Not many kids can do that.'

"We laughed about that the rest of the day. From then on, when any of the boys did something special, we would say, 'Not many kids can do that!'" As circumstances catapulted our family from one musical achievement to another, we found themselves referring back again and again to that moment and that statement and how prophetic it had become.

Mother had to have a schoolroom in the new house. That was a "must." But there was just no room for it. The dining room had been serving temporarily, but that would never do in the long run. After thinking it over for several weeks, she decided that the high-pitched attic roof had a lot of space where they could build a very large room. However, there was no way to get up to the attic except for a small trap door in the ceiling. So, one day while Father was on a business trip, Mother had a contractor come over and build a set of stairs in the dining room that went from the kitchen door up to the attic.

She waited nervously throughout the day when Father would return home and find the new stairs. "I watched as he came through the door, walked into the dining room and right past the stairs and into the kitchen. There were a couple of minutes of silence, and then he stuck his head out of the kitchen door, looked at the stairs and asked, 'Whaaaat is that?!'

"The boys and I laughed, and we all began to talk at once and tell him about the idea for the attic school room. It didn't take George long to see what a great idea it was and he jumped right into the project."

After the room was built, Father bought another 9' x 6" piece of plywood, painted the slick side with blackboard paint and hung it on the north wall. He also put a chalk ledge underneath it like he had done at the Third Street house. Next, he found some desks that had once been in a school, and he bought five of them.

From a school catalogue, Mother ordered sets of the alphabet to put around the room close to the ceiling. One was the printed alphabet, and the other was the Palmer method alphabet which helped us practice writing in that method.

The blackboard was multi-functional and used to teach us addition, subtraction and our times tables. We also loved to draw pictures, so Mother bought us chalk in different colors. Again they painted the shelves they built in the same color themes as before—red, blue, yellow, etc.

Though it was built for school work, the attic eventually became a music room, as well, where Father taught my brothers how to sing and my mother gave us all saxophone lessons.

"Virl and Tom continued learning to talk with the Maico 'Train-ear' unit and they were making great progress with their speech," Mother recorded. "We used our meal times to help them. We made sure that they never felt embarrassed when we corrected them. We were careful to praise their accomplishments first and then make 'suggestions' on how they could improve even more. They knew we did this because we cared about them. And it was interesting to see how each one of us had a different way of working with them.

"For example, Tom was having trouble saying a 'J' properly. Alan suggested Tom put his hand on his throat so he could feel the vibrations of his voice, and then showed him how to hold his teeth tightly together and make the 'J' sound. This was something I had not thought of doing before."

Once my father bought our cow, Pansy, he took me and Tom out to the barn and showed us the right and wrong way to milk her. After getting stepped on and having the milk bucket tip over a few times, I finally got the hang of it and got the job—permanently. My mother would not let the family drink unpasteurized milk, so she bought a pasteurizing unit from the Sears catalogue that would process two gallons of milk at a time. Our family pediatrician reinforced her decision that she should not let us drink unpasteurized milk because of bacteria dangers. I remember we first put the milk through a separator to remove the cream. Then we would pour the remaining milk into the metal pasteurizing container. A metal rod went down into the milk to heat it, and when it reached a certain temperature, it would buzz.

Mom would then remove the inner container, put a plug in the top, set it in the bathtub and run cold water over it. When it was cool, she poured it into half-gallon Mason jars and put it in the refrigerator. With the cream, she would churn butter and make ice cream. (She was a wonderful cook.) I can still remember the smooth, rich taste of the ice cream. Nothing like it exists in stores today. It was fresh from the cow! Each of us boys would take a shift turning the crank on the ice cream machine and keeping it full of ice. Our anticipation was almost overwhelming as we waited for it to be done and then fought for a turn to lick the churning paddle.

Our little farm was our school, our playground, and our metaphor for life. From harvesting apples to hoeing weeds out of the potato patch, Father and Mother would turn it into a learning moment. My father would apply everything we did to our future lives by saying, "Now, when you grow up...," and then he would explain to us how the principle of cleaning out the barn was the same principle as keeping all work spaces clean. Whatever trade we chose, we should keep our work space clean, so we could be more productive. He convinced us that our cow gave more milk, because the barn was tidy.

Mother would always apply everything to the gospel. Barn cleaning was a lesson on the importance of keeping yourself morally and spiritually clean.

Oh, we were like other kids, No one wanted to get up at five in the morning and hoe sugar beets before school. But our complaints were pointless. Father would pull rank on us, get into a military mode and start calling us to attention. Mother would quote scripture about the prodigal son or some other gospel story. From feeding our dog, Tip, to mowing the lawn, every aspect of our home was a learning experience.

Even in our chores, Father applied his military training to organize it. When it came to washing the dishes for example, Mother would wash, Father would rinse, and we boys would line up with towels and take turns drying a dish, putting it away and then getting in line to dry another dish again. Henry Ford was not as organized as my parents!

As I said earlier, just when things seemed to be running along smoothly for our family, something would come along to disrupt the peace. My mother wrote: "My parents had some real health problems which caused me a lot of anxiety. Mother had been very delicate most of her life. She had appendicitis when she was young, but the doctors did not seem to know what was causing her problems. She finally had it removed when I was just a little girl, and the doctor said it had ruptured several times and scarred over. He did not know how she had ever survived. She also had her gall bladder removed, and she had problems with her heart. In addition, she suffered with eczema, and her hands were often sore and cracked.

Dad had an enlarged heart from rheumatic fever which he had suffered when he was a child. He also had a severe case of asthma. He took a lot of medicine to try and help his situation."

Among my mother's possessions are several letters she wrote to her father when he was hospitalized. They are examples of her love and devotion for him.

Here are some excerpts: "To my wonderful dad: I did not sleep much last night for thinking about you up there in the hospital—wishing I could stay right by your side for the week you have to stay there. I have often wished we had more time for each other. Anyway, I want you to know that I love you very dearly, and I am so proud of you. You are just all that any dad could be. I know I should tell you these things more often.

"As I look back over my childhood, all I can remember is happiness. I think of the hours you and I spent together on the farm riding around on the tractor with you and having you as my teacher in grades 5, 6, 7 and 8 at the District #61 schoolhouse. I remember Mom teaching me how to keep accounting books, play the piano, make quilt blocks, can fruit, etc. Oh, how I would love to live those days over. But the purpose of life is to move forward, so I guess we should try more from now on to make new happy memories.

"I imagine it makes parents happy to see their grown-up children happy, too. And I am still one of the happiest girls in the world. I'm so grateful for my wonderful little sons and my dear husband. The Lord has again blessed me immensely. I feel sometimes that I should devote the rest of my life working in the Church to show Him how I appreciate all my blessings. I doubt if I would appreciate these things so much if I had not had such wonderful parents. I remember you kneeling in prayer a lot and how it impressed me when I was little. I remember how humble you were when my little brother, Tom, was born."

Another excerpt: "All those shots should be taking hold about now and clearing that infection from your system. That was a wonderful prayer and blessing Bishop Wimmer gave you last night. I have faith all those things he said in your blessing will come true.

"I did not get up quite so early this morning, and as a result, I have to rush to get the 'fellers' ready for school. They were all up in the night for some reason (except Virl and Merrill). The others came piling in bed with us at different intervals and had to be settled down. About the time I would get one settled, the other would wake up. I did not hear the alarm this morning. George got up and shut it off and let me sleep an extra five.

And one more: "Daddy, I woke up early this morning thinking about you—how much I love you—and how wonderful you've always been—and I had to have a good cry. I have worried so much about you being sick that I believe I have relived almost every incident in our lives together. I remember how I used to 'tag' around with you on the farm and bring you lemonade—and when I would get lonesome, I would go out and watch you go 'round and 'round the field plowing on the tractor. What a thrill I'd get when you let me ride on it with you.

"I remember how patient you were in letting me sit on your lap and drive the car—and how you used to carefully carry me into the house when I went to sleep when driving home late at night. (Sometimes I was not even asleep, either. I sometimes played possum and enjoyed your just carrying me into the house. Being in your arms made me feel so secure.)

"I remember you going to all your Church meetings and coming home and telling us of the wonderful Spirit that was there, and how you enjoyed it. I have always been happy when I saw you happy. I am grateful to think you and Mother live close to me, and I can see you for a few minutes every once in awhile. I want you to take good care of yourselves, so I can have you for a long, long, time. I just feel that there are a lot of happy days for us together doing temple work and genealogy."

Mother always tried to get up about an hour earlier than the rest of our family, so she could plan her day, read the scriptures, and study nutrition and other subjects. She became intensely focused on keeping her family healthy. She was especially intrigued by the information found in Mormon scripture, *Doctrine and Covenants*, called the "Word of Wisdom." It was a law of health given to the Prophet Joseph Smith by the Lord for the benefit of the church. Besides explaining that alcohol, tobacco and hot drinks, such as coffee and tea, are not good for man, it also talks about foods that are not healthy and others that are good for you. It puts wheat at the top of the healthy list and promises health to those who live this law.

As I said, My mother was influenced by a book called *The Healthy Hunzas*. It said they ate very little meat, and when they did eat it, the women would use it to make stew. In that stew, they would throw in handfuls of wheat. So she asked George to buy a big wheat grinder, and every morning he would coarsely grind some for their hot breakfast cereal. And about three times a week, he would grind it even finer so she could make loaves of whole wheat bread. From then on, everything that my mother made had wheat in it. Even cookies and cakes had wheat. We got used to baked goods being brown.

Mother also learned that apricots were loaded with Vitamin A, which is an anti-infection vitamin, and since we had a lot of apricots on our trees, she used to bottle them or dry them in the sun. Once they were dry, she wrapped them in freezer paper and froze them. "Then, when the boys wanted a little snack after school or had a 'sweet tooth,'" she wrote, "they could get a little sack of 'candy-cots,' and I knew they were eating something good for them. The boys also loved to blend the apricots with pineapple juice and ice cubes and wanted it almost every morning with their breakfast."

My mother continued her love of reading throughout most of her life. Her reading took her ahead of the times, not only as a real estate broker, but in so many areas. What she read, she put into practice, whether it was practical information or spiritual insights. She kept notebooks of quotes and information she had read and would file them under the appropriate subject matter. Mother learned shorthand during the war, and a large number of her study notes were written in it. Every book she read had her annotations in the margin spaces.

But Mother did not keep all this knowledge to herself. She would find every opportunity to share it with us and explain it to us. She would hang thoughts and quotes on the refrigerator, the doors and the bathroom mirror. In the years to come, as we all got married and had families of our own, she was still sharing her knowledge with us in her "Memos From Mother," a newsletter that she would regularly send to each of us. She even started a version of it in the Osmond Fan Club which she sent to all the fans that signed up for it. When she started her own publishing company, she called it Knowledge Unlimited. It was dedicated to printing and distributing books that would teach and uplift, as is this book.

Christmas preparations when we lived at "two-twenty-eight" were always started several months ahead of time. My parents did not buy many toys and trinkets for us during most of the year. Even birthdays were kept relatively simple. But at Christmas time, Mother bought items with money that she had saved up all year long. This was no easy chore, managing a Christmas list for all those boys. But in October, the new Sears Christmas catalogue arrived, and, one by one, each boy would turn its sacred pages and discover new wonders to dream about and mark as part of their wish list. Mother would take note, and then quietly, an order would be sent in. When the package arrived, she discreetly hid it away along with the other packages, all over the house. So, by the time December arrived, all that was left for her to do was to buy surprises for stockings and manage the preparation for the smorgasbord.

It became traditional to decorate the family Christmas tree on December first (their wedding anniversary). Then Mother would start to place packages under the tree—just a few at a time—which increased everyone's curiosity and excitement.

"We also decorated other parts of the house," she wrote. "Virl was usually in charge of that because he was the artistic one. He also made lists of things that had to be done. He gave out assignments, so that the whole month of December was filled to the brim with activities. He made sure everything was organized."

Mother always made pajamas for everyone. They were put under the tree in a special place where we could open them on Christmas Eve.

Whenever we had any special holiday or activity, my father would always line us up by seniority, like a set of graduated columns, and he would take the appropriate photos for our memory album. As we got older and 8mm movie cameras became available, my father would be ready with that camera, too. Again he would line us up according to age and have us make a grand entrance into the room.

Father had this big, bright floodlight he would set up when taking the movies of us. He would line us up, turn that thing on, and then yell, "Okay, come down the stairs, and everyone act natural!" But that was hard to do when we had that light in our faces. So all of our Christmas footage had us squinting and shading our eyes with our hands.

The excitement of opening our presents was unreal. Each year one of the boys was assigned to sit by the tree and hand out the gifts. We tried to keep that orderly too, but it was nearly impossible. In the end, it became a free-for-all. There were plenty of packages under the tree, but Santa Claus never wrapped the things he left. He just had tags attached to everything with our names on them.

Our maternal grandparents added to the excitement. In fact, most of the time they were the ones who would be up first and would wake up the family very early in the morning.

One of my Father's favorite holiday songs was "I Just Go Nuts at Christmas" by Yogi Yorgason. Every holiday, he would sing at least one rendition of it with Mother at the piano. And he always surprised her with some last minute shopping. In fact, "last minute" was how Father did most of his holiday shopping. I remember once he bought Mother a lovely crystal necklace and earrings and snuck them under the tree. Mother cried when she opened them.

"As soon as the gifts were unwrapped, we each made a pile of our 'stuff,' so Father could take more pictures. Then we would throw away the papers, boxes, etc., and Father would make us put our gifts away, so the house would be clean again. Then it was time to begin preparing the smorgasbord with all its fragrant delicacies. The house was filled with wonderful smells. Mother made homemade chocolates for Christmas, but they were so good that a lot of them never made it to Christmas Day. It was a magical time.

Mother wrote about her boys in her journal nearly daily—how they were growing, things they did. Here are some entries: "Virl is very artistic. The drawings he brings home from school are beautiful—especially the perspective drawings of buildings. His ideas are so creative and modern. He also does detailed drawings of space ships that he imagines.

"Tom is so loving and tries to be so patient with us. But he gets mad when we all talk at once, because he cannot figure out who is saying what. Then he will stop us and say, 'Hey, remember that I am deaf! Look at me when you talk, so I can understand you!' We really need to be more considerate and thoughtful for his sake so he doesn't feel left out.

"Alan became attached to a little doll when he was two years old. One day the head broke off of it and George threw it away. I don't know how he got it, but the next day, there was Alan holding onto that doll's head. There was no separating him from it. He had to have it on his bed whenever he went to sleep.

"Wayne wore little suspenders to hold his pants up when he was a little boy. He would pull those suspenders up so tight the waist would be up near his armpits. But that was the only way he would wear them. It must have made him feel more secure. He loved wearing this little cowboy hat all the time, too.

"George had a nickname for Wayne. He called him 'Wonky Donky.' Where he came up with that, I do not know, but Wayne seemed to enjoy it, so we used it often. One day, a fellow from the feed store delivered some grain for our cow, and, as he walked into the house to bring me the bill, he turned to Wayne and said, 'What's your name, young man?' 'Wonky Donky' was the reply. The look on the man's face told me maybe we better start calling him Wayne.

"Merrill is the happiest baby that I have ever seen. He is always giggling at everything. He likes to make funny faces too and to tease all the other boys. To Merrill, life is just simply humorous."

As always, the family grew once again. "My beloved sixth son, Jay Wesley Osmond was born in the Dee Hospital, Ogden, Utah on March 2, 1955. I made yellow blankets for his bassinet, because I needed something other than blue for a change.

"When Jay was about 1-1/2 years old, I upholstered a little chair for him. I don't remember where we got the chair but it was a miniature of the overstuffed, upholstered-type chairs with the big arms. It was cute but needed recovering. I bought some material with a gray background and a tiny black and red design on it and covered it with that. Jay was so delighted with that chair! He crawled in and out of it time and time again. He would just get seated, then he would crawl out again, turn around, stand up in it, crawl over the arms, twist around and sit back down.

"George bought a small organ for our wedding anniversary. Virl could hear the notes on it better than he could on the piano. He loved to sit on the organ bench and play the keys. One day I noticed that Tom was sitting by the side of the organ and leaning his ear against it while I played. I stopped to see what would happen. After a few minutes he would look around at me and say, 'More.' He could feel the vibrations of the music, and would bob his head to the beat.

"Tom did not benefit from a hearing aid as much as Virl did in those days, because he was so profoundly deaf, and the hearing aids just were not strong enough. He could feel sounds more than hear them. But Virl could hear sounds with his hearing aid box pressed close to the organ. He begged me to teach him to play it. I helped him to learn a couple of hymns. Once he understood that the musical notes represented keys on the organ, he continued to teach himself and even helped Tom to learn how to play it."

It was at this time that Father discovered some of his boys really liked to sing. He had a beautiful voice and, to pass the time in the car when we were traveling, he used to sing songs to us. Soon my brothers would learn the songs and sing with him. One time he told the boys to sing the melody, and he would sing the harmony. The boys loved that.

Once he heard Alan singing the harmony, too, while the other boys continued to sing the melody. He was stunned. Father had always liked barbershop songs and the rich four-part harmony. He had even sung in a local barbershop group himself. His mind raced. Could he teach Alan, Wayne, Merrill and Jay to sing like that?

My mother had already taken out her saxophone and was teaching each of us boys how to play it, along with the piano. Music was already at part of our family.

But this—this was different. Jay was only one-and-a-half when Father started to introduce the boys to the concept of singing in harmony. It became a part of their "chores" to spend time each day with him, learning how to sing.

While Mother played the piano, Father taught them both individually and as a group. For the boys, it was a game—they just had fun singing with Father. But, by the time Jay was three, they had improved and learned so much that Father knew they were "ready."

So, my mother had her time of relative domestic bliss at "two twenty-eight." Her parents' health improved, and Father did not come home with another "deal that can't be passed up." But he had other ideas on his mind. Little did she know how much her husband's singing instructions were going to change the lives of the whole family.

OLIVE OSMOND

SIX LITTLE FARMERS

BARBERSHOP BOYS

CHAPTER THIRTEEN
BARBERSHOP

My mother was thirty years old when Jay was born. In that same year, she became ill with a kidney infection. She was running a high temperature and felt very faint, so she went to see her doctor. He took blood tests and he told her that her white blood cell count was very low. He sent her home and told her if she did not feel better the next day, she was to let him know.

The following morning she was so weak, she nearly passed out, so she called him again, and he ordered her to the hospital where they gave her sulfa drugs and did blood tests every morning for several days. But her condition never changed, so she begged the doctor to let her go home and be with her six little boys. They were being cared for by their aunt, because her parents were on a trip to California. The doctor relented and released her. Once home, the phone rang. Father answered it in his office at the same time that Mother picked it up in the kitchen. She overheard the doctor say to Father, "George, you have a very sick wife."

"What do you mean? How sick is she?"

"I'd give her about six weeks to live if the situation doesn't improve," was the grim reply.

Mother said that the blood rushed out of her face. She hung up the phone and stumbled into her bedroom and shut the door. She sat on her bed as tears streamed down her cheeks.

Typically, she was not thinking of herself. She started repeating, "My babies, my babies…." She slipped down on her knees by her bed and pleaded with the Lord. "Dear Father in Heaven, don't let me die. Not yet. Let me live long enough to raise my children."

On Sunday Mother and Father fasted and prayed and then called a family friend to come and assist in giving her a blessing. Before the blessing, Father asked her, "Olive, do you have faith the Lord can heal you?"

Mother replied, "I don't doubt that if the Lord wants me to live, I will."

Then he said, with loving conviction in his voice, "There is enough faith in this room to heal you if you desire." And they laid their hands on her head and gave her the sought-after blessing.

"Immediately I felt a 'power' of some kind travel through my body, and right out the end of my toes," my mother wrote.

"A couple of days later I told George I felt much better and would like to go get another blood test. (I already had one scheduled for next Friday, but I wanted one sooner.) He suggested I wait for my appointment, but I insisted, so he said, 'Okay, call the doctor.' The doctor responded in the same manner, 'Well, you have an appointment Friday—give yourself a chance.'

"I insisted that I felt better and needed to know.'"

He relented and Mother had her blood drawn and then waited in his office until the results from the lab came in. "The phone rang and when the doctor answered, he just stared at me with a peculiar look on his face. I thought I was doomed," she wrote.

"But then he said, 'Do you realize that you're out of danger?!' I told him about the blessing I received, and he said, 'I believe you, because there's no other way this could have happened!'"

About a year later, when she met him on the street in Ogden, he exclaimed, "I can't believe you're still walking around. You are really a miracle. I saw case after case like yours when I practiced in Boston, and they were all fatal!' (She had been diagnosed as having had aplastic anemia.)

After receiving the good news that her prayers had been answered, Mother said she again got on her knees to thank the Lord for listening to her pleas for help and promised to serve the Lord faithfully all the rest of her life for having been given this gift. She kept her promise.

"The next summer, we decided to take our family on a vacation to Yellowstone National Park," wrote Mother. "As we were traveling along, George and I started singing the barbershop song, 'The Old Oaken Bucket' together. I sang lead, and he took a harmony part. Alan hushed the other boys and said, 'Listen to Father! Listen to Father!' Then he leaned forward close to George, so he could learn his notes and was soon singing the harmony part along with him.

Wayne wanted to try it too, so George said, 'Let's sing a third part then.' He started singing another part, while Alan continued to sing the new harmony he had learned. Merrill was interested in learning too, so they taught each other. We sang 'The Old Oaken Bucket' all the way to Yellowstone Park and back."

Mother and Father both loved barbershop harmony. Friends had taken them to a barbershop convention in Ogden the year before. The organization is known as the SPEBSQSA. (The Society for the Preservation and Encouragement of Barber Shop Quartet Singing in America).

When they got back from their trip, Mother went to the music store and bought several books of arrangements for quartets. "We started with just using three-part harmony," she wrote. "The first song they worked on was 'I Want a Girl Just Like the Girl That Married Dear Old Dad.' I also selected several hymns that they could sing at church, such as "Prayer Is the Key to Heaven, But Faith Unlocks the Door.' I would record each part separately on the same wire recorder we had purchased to assist Virl and Tom with their speech. Then, at night, when I tucked the boys in, I would play each part over a few times to help them learn their individual notes. Then I would shut off the recorder and see how well they could harmonize on their own. They enjoyed this and began to develop a good ear for harmonizing together."

The word soon got out that my brothers were singing together. It was not long before they were asked to sing in church programs and dinners. They literally "sang for their supper" on many occasions.

"People would ask me, 'How do you get your boys to practice?' George and I would exchange glances and just smile, because we knew that was the easiest part of the whole thing. Alan, Wayne, Merrill and Jay loved to sing and harmonize. Sometimes we would actually have to make them quit singing, so they could get some sleep!"

Soon my brothers went from singing in church to watching barbershop quartets and trying to imitate them. They now called themselves The Osmond Brothers, and were invited to perform at the annual convention of the Barbershop Quartet Society. Their performance was not for competition but for a novelty. However, they got a standing ovation from the judges, the audience and other competitors with their rendition of "Ragtime Cowboy Joe."

As our family focus became more and more geared toward music, Tom and I began to feel a bit isolated. The more they practiced and went to sing in competitions, the more the farm chores fell upon us. Tom and I never said much about our feelings to the rest of the family, but we talked about it together in private.

"Why are we deaf so that we cannot sing with our brothers and make our parents proud of us, too?"

We were starting to feel lost. Our secure, happy, organized lives were changing. There was a new focus and passion that we could not be a part of. It was the first time in my life that I think I became aware of what it was to be depressed. Up until that point, being deaf had not really mattered.

Then, one evening, as we were all driving home from a competition, my parents and younger brothers were talking excitedly about the experience and their future plans. Tom sat quietly, staring out the car window. Under my breath, I said to myself, "I wish I had some talent."

I did not notice my mother's reaction. I did not even think that she heard me. But later she wrote in her journal, "My heart was broken. We had worked so hard teaching Alan, Wayne, Merrill and Jay that I had allowed myself to become blind to the needs and feelings of my two oldest sons. I shed so many tears that night trying to figure out how to include Virl and Tom in this musical whirlwind we were involved in."

The next day, my mother announced to Tom and me that she had enrolled us in tap dancing lessons. It was all about rhythm, routine and coordination. Even if we could not hear the music well—or not at all—we could feel the beat and count timing. Tom and I loved it. I think somewhere inside we knew that it was just a chance for us to express ourselves musically, but that it was never going to lead down the same path our brothers were on. Still we embraced it with enthusiasm. Later, when my brothers' act required that they be more visual and active on stage, Tom and I taught them some tap routines.

Mother kept opening opportunities for Tom and me. She continued to teach us the basic rudiments of the saxophone and the piano right up until music became a career for my brothers and not just a hobby. Then time constraints on my mother made it less and less possible for her to keep tutoring us.

In spite of my brothers' singing successes, there was still a business to run and bills to be paid. Mother decided to open a little dress boutique and call it LaVerna's Dress Shop, named after my father's mother. At this time Father was appointed Postmaster of the Five Points Post Office even though he still had his real estate and insurance agency. Then he was called to be second counselor to our ward bishop (pastor) at church. This volunteer position had him gone a great deal at night and on weekends serving in the church.

But we continued to make our Family Night time sacred and carried on with that tradition with even more vigilance. And Father kept our family more tightly organized than before. We each knew our duties and responsibilities, and Father's word was law. Sometimes people would suggest that we were too organized and did not have enough downtime, but as I look back, I know my father was meant to be the strong leader of our family. Without his firm hand, my brothers never would have accomplished what they did.

But Father's patriarchal position in the family and increasing tough hand did not stop my mother from wringing her hands at times with concern. Mother was my brothers' greatest champion, but, as they became more and more successful, the pressure to perform better increased with it. The game of singing with Father became more serious. He would not allow the boys to "goof off" when practicing or at a performance. Associations with friends became limited as they focused on performance. My mother once agonizingly wrote, "My boys sing so beautifully, but I am so worried they are trading their childhood for it. George works them so hard. It's like the boys have become another business. Are we doing the right thing?"

Like every challenge in my mother's life, she turned to prayer for answers and guidance. Father would brush her off if she suggested to him that he was being too hard on the boys. She had to know for sure that they were on the right path. In prayer, the Spirit suggested to her heart that she should attend the temple, and there she would receive the answer she sought. A temple is the most sacred place on earth to Mormons. It is considered the House of the Lord. It is where each worthy church member receives the most important and sacred ordinances, and it is a place of pure revelation.

So there is where she went to seek the will of the Lord. When she came home, she wrote in her journal, "Now I know for sure that the Lord has a special mission for my sons, and that George was supposed to be their father and guide and direct them in pursuit of that destiny. I am no longer afraid. I am at peace,"

And in the midst of this flurry of activity, Mother gave birth to her seventh son Donald Clark Osmond on December 9, 1957, 12:55 a.m., at the same hospital as the other children.

"I ordered him all these cute little clothes through LaVerna's Dress Shop. He was a darling and a sweet addition to our family—we were happy as larks."

In the seventh grade, I attended Mound Fort Junior High School in Ogden. The year before I had tried going to the Utah School for the Deaf with Tom—more for an experiment to see if I would like it better and learn more by getting personal attention from the teachers. The staff there, however, felt I had sufficient hearing to get along well enough in regular junior high, so I went back there.

I no longer wore the hearing aid box strapped to my chest. Technology had improved, and now I had two behind-the-ear hearing aids that were attached to a pair of black horned-rim glasses with little cords that went into plugs in my ears. Better than the box, but the glasses did not do much for my self-esteem.

Tom continued to attend the deaf school. His profound hearing loss and continual struggle with speech acquisition made it impossible for him to function in a hearing scholastic environment.

My younger brothers continued to attend local school as well, even though my father frequently took them out to perform and attend barbershop competition, much to the consternation of the principles and teachers. But Mother worked with the schools, getting lessons from classes and teaching the boys at home or on the road herself, so they could keep up.

The Ogden School for the Deaf always made big deal of Halloween. They had a party, activities and, best of all, a "Spook Alley" which the students made. One day we decided to do the same thing at home by setting up a spook alley in the upstairs schoolroom.

"Virl and Alan fixed up a gruesome scene," Mother wrote. "They stuffed a pair of George's old pants and shirt and laid it on a plank. They then put this ghastly mask on its head and added a hat and shoes. It would really give you a start to walk in there. Then they hung a large black bolt from the ceiling, so it would swing when the door was opened. It was supposed to be a spider."

BARBERSHOP

Granted, our first attempt at this Halloween tradition was less then inspiring. But every year it became a passion to build another bigger, better spook alley. It was a way for my brothers to kick back and unwind. Before show business had them traveling so much that they were never home for Halloween, we would use black lights, record creepy sounds and create mechanical gadgets that moved and groaned. We would dress up like ghouls and monsters and scare the wits out of the local children in the neighborhood. It was fun, and our parents were good sports about it.

In spite of all the musical practices and scheduling our family had to manage, Mother and Father tried to keep life as normal as they could for us at home. There were still family nights, along with family prayer and scripture study. There were chores and school. And of course, Mother was pregnant again.

But this was not just any pregnancy! On October 13, 1959, my mother Olive gave birth to her first and only girl, Olive Marie Osmond. And what made it so special is that she arrived on my father's birthday! Now, up until that time, fathers were not allowed in the delivery room, so my father was used to the routine of hanging out in the waiting room, and he was perfectly content to continue that tradition. But, as they wheeled my mother to the deliver room, she grabbed his arm and said, "You are coming with me!" So he put on hospital gear and came into delivery.

"I had dreamed that I was going to have a boy named James Arthur Osmond," she penned in her journal. "I was shocked when the doctor told me it was a girl! But no one was more shocked than George. He had seven sons and all he knew how to raise were sons. Now on his birthday of all things, he got his first girl.

"Before I went to the hospital to have Marie, Tom had peeked around the door and said, 'Mother have a baby girl, I hope.' When the word reached the family that I did, Father dressed all seven of the boys alike and took them to the hospital to 'serenade' me and Marie. They sang, 'I Want A Girl Just Like The Girl that Married Dear Dear Old Dad.' The nurses on the floor cried, and one them called the *Ogden Examiner* newspaper about it. They, in turn, phoned George to have the boys repeat the performance for the newspaper photographer.

"I wondered why I had the dream about another boy. Then I realized that I was told this (about Jimmy), so that we would not stop having children once I got my beloved daughter. I now knew there was one more up there that was coming to us."

Mother did not mention this "other" child to my father for awhile. She just let him get used to the idea that he had a daughter. Then a year later, she told him about that dream and explained she felt there was one more spirit in heaven that needed to come to them. Father looked at her and said: "Olive, we have eight kids! But if you want one more, then go right ahead. It is not going to make much difference at this point!"

JIMMY & OLIVE

OLIVE OSMOND

OSMOND BROTHERS PLUS DONNY
(Andy Williams Show)

CHAPTER FOURTEEN

STARDOM

How our family fussed over Marie. The boys loved to carry her around at home and at church. Mother dressed her like a little doll. She pulled out all those dresses she had stored in the cedar chest. Those, along with the ones she sewed for her daughter, lifted her into sheer ecstasy. She finally had her baby girl.

As for my brothers and me, having a little sister around was quite a curiosity. We took every opportunity to see what she would do in different situations. Figuring out how girls acted was a constant mystery to us. Once we discovered that if you spilled something on the floor, little two-year-old Marie would go get a towel and clean it up. We wore her out with that trick. In everything she did, she was "different," and we were "confused."

Donny figured her out best. They became pals and got into a lot of mischief together. Once Mother found them sitting in their closet rubbing peanut butter all over each other!

During this school year, Tom became obsessed with increasing his vocabulary. Mother wrote, "He carries a red dictionary under his arm most of time reading and reciting words and challenging all of us to spell them or guess their meaning. It seems every time we sat down to the dinner table, Tom would take out that dictionary and start testing us."

Alan learned to play the bass violin at this point, and Father brought home a drum set for us boys. Even Tom and I had fun with that instrument. Mother wrote, "Television was available now, and George bought the family our first black and white TV. He made the boys watch every performer on the different variety shows and would point out techniques that they used."

They especially followed the Lennon Sisters, another family singing group on the Lawrence Welk Show. They definitely were gearing up for the next stage in their musical life. They learned a new song to perform for each family night. Mother put a motto on the wall in the kitchen that read: "Prepare yourself, and the opportunity will come."

At night, when my brothers and I were all in bed, I would listen to Alan, Wayne Merrill and Jay talking about a performance that they had just done and what they would do different the next time. They would be both nervous and excited about their next competition.

Sometimes we would talk about school or the farm, but more and more their life was music. It was during this time that Tom and I started to teach our brothers some basics of the American Sign Language. We taught them how to finger spell and gave them several other signs. Then we would test them during our night time conversations. Learning sign language became an important tool for them later in show business. They could be on opposite sides of the stage from each other and without saying a word, they could communicate directions. They used it a lot.

"The popularity of the boys is spreading," Mother wrote. "They went to Kansas City, to the Muehlebach Hotel to perform. Merrill sang a solo called, 'Take Me Back to Babyland.' In the audience was an elderly man who had written the song. After Merrill finished singing, the audience was very quiet for a minute. Mr. Rooney was in tears, he had been so touched by Merrill's rendition of his song. Finally someone in the audience said, 'Don't kids play with toys any more?' Then the audience broke into applause."

Mother heard the Evans Quartet on the radio one day. They had just won the International Barbershop Championship in Chicago. This was another talented group of family singers. "I did not see why my sons could not join the local chapter of SPEBSQSA, so I called them. I was told that they were too young to be in it. But they did invite us to the next meeting. I told George and we decided to take the boys and go."

As it turned out, this meeting was to be a welcome home for Evans Quartet which was from Utah. The boys were invited to sing several songs at the meeting, and the members of the quartet were so impressed that they invited them to sing in Brigham City with them. "We were very excited."

They went on to sing in the mountain community of Huntsville, Utah for the Sons of the Mormon Pioneers. The prophet of the church, David O. McKay, lived in Huntsville. He invited our family to his home. President McKay looked every bit the part of a prophet. He was in his eighties—tall with a thick shock of white hair. He radiated love, kindness, warmth and compassion, and he loved music. The boys sang for him, and he exclaimed afterwards, "What a great group of missionaries!"

Looking at me, he said, "You are the oldest. You'll probably go on a mission first. (He did not know that I was hearing impaired. No one had ever been called to go on a mission with this disability.) He then opened his wallet and gave me a five dollar bill for my future mission. I never spent it. I still have it in my possession. Later, I actually did get the opportunity to go on a mission. I was the first "deaf" missionary for the Church of Jesus Christ of Latter-day Saints.

Huntsville is located twelve miles east of Ogden up Ogden Canyon at about five thousand feet. Mother and Father thought it was lovely up there and very peaceful. They expressed interest in buying some property there.

After the boys performed, a man approached Father with an offer to take them to a lot he had for sale. They saw it and immediately liked it. They bought it and had a basement home built on it just like the first one that they had ever built.

"We loved the fact that the property overlooked the lake and that there was a pond in back too," wrote Mother. "We told ourselves we would build the upper level of our dream home later on."

Even though we finally did build a complete home in Huntsville, we never really lived there. It became like a summer home for us. We planted a willow tree by the pond and put in raspberry bushes and harvested a couple of gardens, but my parents never really put in the effort to fix this place up the way they had done with other homes. They could not. Their time and focus was on Alan, Wayne, Merrill, Jay and music. But we had great times there anyway. My brothers and I would take our B.B. guns, line up cans and sit on the back porch and shoot at them. We would paddle canoes in the pond and fish in the lake. It was wonderful to run and play and just be boys.

It was one thing to sing in small communities in Utah, and it was quite another to break into the big-time. In the spring we learned that there was a barbershop convention in Pasadena, California. The Evans Quartet encouraged my brothers to attend. And most importantly, the Evans Quartet was going to be there, and we learned that they had been invited to sing on the Lawrence Welk Show. They said that they would introduce the family to him.

This was the first time that my parents traveled together with my brothers and left Tom and me at home with our grandparents in Utah. Only then did Tom and I realize how different our lives were destined to be. Mother cried when she kissed us goodbye. She kept saying she was so sorry we could not go. Normally it had been Father who traveled with the boys, and Mother would stay home with us and the little kids.

"Father needs me to help him this time. It is just a few days and then we will be back. I promise." But in her eyes I saw the strain and worry and anticipation of pursuing this exciting direction and trying to make us feel a part of it. "You are my special sons and I love you so much," she said as they went out the door.

As it turned out, they never did meet Lawrence Welk. But they did meet the Lennon Sisters and their father, Bill. They graciously invited the family to their home. The Lennon Sisters Quartet was the eldest four in a family of twelve siblings, so they could relate to the Osmonds. The boys sang for the Lennon Family. Mrs. Lennon kept saying, "Lawrence has to hear these kids."

While waiting to get an appointment with Lawrence Welk, the family stayed at the Lennon's' beach house overnight. The next day Father took the boys to Disneyland to meet the barbershop quartet called The Dapper Dans. They were singing on Main Street.

"George said to the quartet, 'My boys can sing like that!' so the Dapper Dans asked them to perform a song," my mother wrote. "Tommy Walker, the director of entertainment, was there. Once he heard the boys sing, Tommy said he could possibly use the boys in July for a show called, 'Disneyland After Dark.' "We'll call you," he said. We were very excited!

"Next it was time to try and meet Lawrence Welk. George got the boys hair combed, and I fussed over their clothes, so they looked bandbox pressed. George had been told to call an 'Uncle Ted' first. But when he called, he was told that Welk was too busy to see them that day. The kids were terribly disappointed. George was frustrated and became fed up with whole business. 'Let's just go home,' he said adamantly,"

Mother, being the positive thinker that she was, said to him: "Oh, George, just roll with the punches. Things are not as bad as they seem." Mother always said that to us when we were having a hard time: "Roll with the Punches." She never let us indulge in self-pity. As far as she was concerned, all the trials of life were manageable, if you had the right attitude.

"On the way back to Ogden, as we drove through Las Vegas, we heard on the radio that Martin Black would like to know if there was anyone with talent out there and he'd put them on his television show. I suggested to George that we drive straight to the television station since we were already in Vegas. He said, 'Mother, you're a doggone extrovert. You are just like a bulldog—you never give up.'

"So, we went. As we walked in, Mimi Heinz was standing there. She and Phil Ford were on the show. She said to us, 'What do we have here, some singers?' I had the boys dressed alike. Mimi fussed over them and took them right to Martin Black. They sang for him, and on the spot, he put them on the show! How the boys loved being on television!

Mimi said, 'You must come to the Desert Inn and see my show. I'll introduce you to Tony Martin.'

"We were on cloud nine! We parked our humble camper in among some Cadillacs in the parking lot, laughed at how silly it looked there, and went in. Tony Martin wept when the boys sang, "I Wouldn't Trade the Silver in My Mother's Hair." He then asked us if we would come back in May and sing on his Mother's Day show. He said he would call us.

"We were so excited as we drove the rest of the way home. The kids practiced so diligently and constantly talked about how they had met the Lennon Sisters and Tony Martin. But we never heard back from him. George tried to call him but could never get through. We were all very disillusioned."

Mother told me that she started making a quilt with Grandma Davis to get her mind off it. Father went back to the office. They still encouraged the boys to pursue their music but things just were not the same as they were before.

Then out of the blue, Tommy Walker called from Disney Entertainment. Could the boys come in July for a part in a Disney movie called, 'The Travels of Jamie McPheaters,' starring Kurt Russell? He said that he would also have the boys sing on Main Street at Disneyland, and they would get *paid*.

"My first intuition was, 'This is it!'" Mother wrote. "Then I realized the logistics of what he was asking us to do. We would be in California for a month."

But complicated logistics never stopped the family, so they rented out our Ogden home on 228 Washington to our aunt and her family and found a manager to handle Father's business. When we had finished packing up our camper and station wagon, Father had us kneel down for a family prayer. He asked the Lord to guide and direct us, and then we all headed west.

Mother said, "I tried to follow George when we arrived in Los Angeles. We had no turn signals on one of the cars, and I was so scared to death on those freeways. We got separated a few times but finally made it to Disneyland."

We parked the camper next to the resort, and the boys reported for work. While the boys entertained at different locations in the park under Father's close supervision, Mother left Donny and Marie in the camper with Tom and me and tried to find a place for us to rent. But no one wanted to rent to a family with eight children. My parents actually considered buying a house out of desperation, since ten people living in a camper and one hotel room was getting uncomfortable.

"George went to a local real estate office, and an agent there said there was house in Santa Ana, whose owner was in Europe. He said he would never know that we had eight kids, so we took it," Mother wrote. "There was no furniture in it, so the agent sent us a couch and a television set. Then I went to the Goodwill Industries nearby and bought us some mattresses, a dining room set, a high chair for Marie and one bed for George and me. The kids slept on mattresses on the floor with bedding we took out of the camper. We were definitely roughing it, but we did not care. We just looked at it as an adventure!

"I loved the dining room set I bought. It was so nice for the family to just sit around and play games. It also served for our school room desks. I bought some clay and art supplies and we sculptured and painted in the back yard.

"Virl, Tom and I practiced our saxophones in this creative environment. Donny and Marie ran around constantly under foot, so I went out and bought a Ken and Barbie doll. Donny did not like the idea of playing with a doll at first, but then he decided that he would be the producer and would create shows for them to perform in. He and Marie spent hours together creating stories that had those dolls living imaginary lives all over the world.

"They were always busy but a little on the mischievous side. I scolded them one day, so they crawled under kitchen table. As I walked in, I heard one of them say, 'She needs some Compose!' This was an over-the-counter tranquilizer being advertised on TV at that time. I decided they were watching too much TV."

In one of the performances the boys did at "Disneyland After Dark," Jay lost his fake mustache during the routine. The boys were very embarrassed about it, but Walt Disney himself had been there and had seen it happen. Still laughing, he said, "Don't change it. Leave it in, leave it in!' So, from then on, it was part of the show.

Besides the barbershop performances my brothers did on Main Street, they also sang at the Golden Horseshoe Review in Frontierland each day. We all loved to go get Sunkist orange juice and ice cream from street vendors, and we rode on the rides every day.

"Disneyland After Dark" was televised live each Saturday night, so the boys got to perform with such great acts as Jack Jones and Louis Armstrong. Then the summer schedule ended. So George approached Tommy Walker and asked him if he would be our manager. His response was, "Would love to, but to be perfectly honest, there's nothing in sight. I'm leaving for Bermuda tomorrow, so it would be unfair to promise you something I don't have. If something comes up, *I'll sure call you.'*"

We were really disappointed to go home this time. Again it was Father who was the first one to be fed up with the fickleness of show business. And it was Mother who encouraged everyone. "There is a purpose for all the experiences we have," she said. "We may not see the purpose now, but the Lord will make it known to us eventually. We just have to have faith."

Because we could not ask our aunt and her family to move out of our Ogden house so quickly, we moved into the basement home in Huntsville, Utah. In the fall, Tom went back to the School for the Deaf, and the boys and I were bussed down the canyon to schools in Ogden. We made plans to build on the upstairs level of the house before the winter set in.

That was in August. In November, we got a call from Jay Williams, who was Andy Williams' father. He saw the boys singing in the Disneyland After Dark show on television, and they reminded him of how the Williams' brothers got their start singing.

Andy Williams and his three older brothers Bob, Don and Dick had formed a quartet called the Williams Brothers in the late 1930's. They first performed on radio in the Midwest. After Andy graduated from high school, he and his brothers appeared with Bing Crosby on the hit record. "Swinging on A Star" (1944).

This led to a nightclub act with entertainer Kay Thompson from 1947 to 1951. Then Andy became a solo act. Eventually, he had a big hit called "Moon River" with Henry Mancini, which sealed his stardom. From there, he was given his own television show.

"Andy was adding new faces to his show all the time," Mother wrote. "So Jay Williams asked George if the boys would audition for Andy. Would we! The boys were going to do a show for SPEBSQSA in San Jose, California the following week anyway.

"As it turned out, Andy was tied up in Hawaii at audition time, so the boys sang for Jay Williams and Andy's brother, Don. We were all so nervous. This was even bigger than Disneyland, and we knew it. The boys practiced hard, and I made sure that every little wrinkle was pressed out of their shirts. The Williams greeted us warmly and put us right at ease. They seemed to really like the boys' performance."

The next day, George took the boys to the SPEBSQSA convention in San Jose. It was their first plane ride. Wayne was especially nervous. That went really well too. And, when they returned, they were finally able to audition for Andy. He loved their act and gave them a spot on two upcoming shows!

"When the time came, our whole family piled back into our old red Mercury station wagon and drove back to Los Angeles with Alan's bass violin strapped to the top. We stayed at a place on Olive Avenue in Burbank. Being a nervous Nelly, I had to call the producers and tell them I had forgotten to pack the boys' red coats. They bought them new navy replacements.

"We had worked hard to bring the boys' career up to this point. We never were sure from one day to the next why we felt so compelled to do it. We just kept praying and holding on to faith that there was a divine purpose in all this.

"When the opportunity came to perform in Disneyland, I thought that was the door or opportunity to stardom. But we went home without an agent or a contract. Now we were back in California, and the boys were to be on Andy Williams' Show twice. And then what? I kept asking the Lord over and over in my prayers to please give me peace about all this.

The first Andy Williams Show my brothers performed on aired December 13, 1962. They made their debut singing, "Be My Little Baby Bumblebee." Mother wrote, "There was so much mail that arrived at the studio after that, saying how cute the boys were and to please have them on again. Andy got the message and right there, he offered us a five-year contract!

"But we could not decide what to do at first. We did not want to be disillusioned again. Should we leave the real estate and insurance businesses after thirteen years of hard work to build it up and throw our kids in show business? George's brother, Rulon, had always been supportive of our performing up until now. When we told him what we were thinking of doing, he said, 'It's foolish! Your kids can sing, but not that good!'

"Everyone discouraged us, except my father, Tom. Somehow he knew all along that we would make it. In fact, he was the one who sent the tape of the boys to Lawrence Welk in the first place. 'Follow your heart and listen to the Lord,' he told me."

"So we did what we always did as a family when we had to make a difficult decision. We made it a matter of prayer. We each tried to set aside our own wants and prejudices and open ourselves to the Lord's will. The answer came through strong and clear to all of us that this was the right thing to do. We took the risk and signed the contract."

So, leaning on their faith, my parents packed up everything again, sold the business in Utah and moved to California and fame. Mother's final comment in her journal at this time was: "We felt we had been called on a mission for the Lord."

OLIVE OSMOND

OLIVE – 16 YEARS OLD

GEORGE AND OLIVE, SERVING AT THE TEMPLE

CONCLUSION

The last of the Osmond children, James Arthur Osmond, was born April 13, 1963. My mother had the baby she had dreamed about. She was thirty-eight. The family was delighted. She said she had given birth to "another tenor."

From there, much of my mother's and my brothers' histories have been recorded. The brothers were groomed and primed for five years on the Andy Williams Show. Then, in 1970, this formerly obscure group of boys from a small Utah town released one simple record called, "One Bad Apple," and shot to worldwide fame.

They took to the road and sang and lifted hearts with their musical talents, while they stood firm in their moral standards and principles. My mother remained ever-vigilant, as their support, counselor and spiritual guide. Yet she reached out beyond her own family and offered a hand of friendship and comfort to people everywhere she went. She was Mother Osmond to fans all over the world.

CONCLUSION

Mother was living with Father in the southern Utah community of St. George, when she suffered a severe stroke. The hospital there did not have the neurological medical personnel to give her the help that she needed, so they life-flighted her to the Utah Valley Regional Medical Center in Provo, Utah.

We were all waiting at the hospital when she arrived. Her CT scan showed a major bleed in the back of her skull. She needed surgery in order to stop it and save her life. We all gathered around her and said a prayer, pleading with the Lord to spare her life. We waited and prayed and talked in hushed tones in the ICU waiting room. When Mother came back from surgery, the doctors said they were fairly confident that they had stopped the bleeding. But, when they took another CT scan, they could see that there was still hemorrhaging occurring in the same area, so the doctors were no longer as confident. They decided they would need to do surgery again. The odds of survival were now lower. Father and all of us children gathered around her bed. We had to make a difficult decision. Father wept. He did not want to see her suffer. So we prayed again, and each of us got the confirmation that we should try and save her life.

They took her into surgery. This time they were successful in stopping the bleeding and stabilizing her condition. We were all relieved, but our relief for her quickly turned into concern for her brother Tom, who had come to the hospital to be with her. Suddenly he collapsed in pain. They rushed him into the emergency room and found that he had a perforated bowel. He, too, was rushed into surgery.

At this time, the first counselor in the Presidency of the Church of Jesus Christ of Latter-day Saints, Thomas S. Monson, came to the hospital to see Mother. He was close friends with our family, so he offered to give both Mother and her brother Tom a healing blessing.

For two weeks, brother and sister lay in adjoining rooms in the ICU fighting for their lives. Both were on ventilators, and both hooked up to numerous monitoring devices. We took turns as a family sitting with Mother twenty-four hours a day, seven days a week. We never left her there alone. Tom's family did the same. But Tom lost his battle and quietly passed away. Mother was unconscious for most of the time and did not learn of his passing for quite awhile.

We waited and we prayed as she began to be regain consciousness. She could not eat, so they put a tube in her stomach. They gave her a breathing tube in her throat, and she was on a ventilator, so she could not talk. Slowly she was able to write us notes. Even then, as she lay there in the hospital, her thoughts were for her family, and she wrote thoughts of encouragement and urged us to remain faithful.

She was in a rehab hospital for one-and-a-half years before she was ever able to come home. The doctors were never able to remove the ventilator or the feeding tube.

I became my father's constant companion as he struggled to deal with my mother's condition. I saw her every day and learned to care for her. We had many intimate conversations at this time, as she wrote to me her testimony of the Lord and shared the details of her life. I lived in their home with Father for the last year of her life and continued to help and care for her.

Then on Mother's Day, May 9, 2004, her kidneys failed, and she quietly passed away. As I sat by her bed holding her hand, I thanked God that I had the privilege of having such a mother and that I could serve her for those two-plus years as she tried to live with dignity and hope after her stroke.

She was loved by people around the world. Flowers and cards came from everywhere. Each of her children spoke at her funeral as did our family friend, Thomas Monson, who said she was not just the Osmonds' mother, but mother to a whole generation of people.

She was as beautiful as she lay in her casket. Her silver hair had been waved the way she had worn it so many times in her life. He face was peaceful and flawless. By her hands were nine gardenias representing each of her children.

At the grave site, I pronounced the dedication, and we all again said one last goodbye. All her grandchildren wrote notes of love to her. These were placed into blue and white helium balloons and released into the sky. Then, like an epitaph from God, two large beautiful butterflies came and circled around the flowers surrounding her casket. They lighted upon them for a brief moment and then lifted up into the heavens and disappeared, guiding my mother's spirit home.

With all my heart, I wish she could have remained with us a little longer. She was our role model, exemplar and provider of endless unconditional love. Father said of her, "Olive is the heart and soul of this family." She was the light and love of my beloved father's life. Just three years later, on November 6, 2007, he followed her home.

When Mother passed away, she left nine children, fifty-five grandchildren and twenty-two great-grand-children. There are many more of us now—all of whom count themselves extraordinarily lucky to have been born into the family of this most inspirational woman.

CONCLUSION

But no one is as grateful as I am to have been her oldest child and to have shared so much time with her. She was the rock upon which I built my life.

ABOUT THE AUTHOR

The author, Virl Osmond, is the oldest of the Osmond children. He is hearing impaired and therefore not one of the performing siblings. He has a degree in Art from Brigham Young University and has been a graphic artist for most of his career. For many years he managed the Osmond Fan Club during the height of his brothers' success. He served as the first deaf Mormon missionary.

He is married to Chris Carroll, and they have seven children. He was both his mother's confidante and one of her primary caretakers during the last years of her life. He experienced a remarkable time with her as she shared her most intimate feelings and stories with him—stories that he now shares in this book.